A LONG WAY FROM FROM PARADISE

The GRAHAM LAWTHER Story

Graham Lawther With James McClelland

AMBASSADOR

A Long Way From Paradise
© Copyright 1991 Graham Lawther and James McClelland

AMBASSADOR PRODUCTIONS LTD.
Providence House
Hillview Avenue,
Belfast BT5 6JR.
U.K.

ISBN 0 907927 65 3

CONTENTS

ACKNOWLEDGEMENTS

This being an autobiography, I must thank those who have helped with my life. If space were to permit I'd list the names of all the faithful ones who ministered to me in Jesus' Name.

My wife Margaret and our children Stephen and Naomi.

Rev. Gordon McDade and the congregation at John White's.

Rev. Jackson Buick and his wife Margaret.

The Staff at E.Y.M. Ministries

The Staff at Prison Fellowship N.I.

James McElroy at T. B. F. Thompson Ministries.

Fred Maguire at Charles Hurst Ltd.

Friends who helped pray this book into being, and my co-author. Please accept my heartfelt thanks.

INTRODUCTION

*"WHEN MY FATHER AND MOTHER FORSAKE ME THEN
THE LORD WILL TAKE ME UP."*
PSALM 27 v 10.

More than twenty five years ago, a wealthy, middle aged businessman used to frequent a rather 'select' night-spot in the city of Belfast, Northern Ireland. A very attractive young woman, in her early thirties, worked there as a barmaid. The businessman wasn't happy or content in his marriage and so, looking for comfort and companionship elsewhere, struck up a relationship with this young woman. How long this relationship lasted no one, except the man, now knows: but of it a child was born. That child was me, Graham Lawther. My mother was Sylvia Lawther.

I never knew my mother - she died when I was just ten months old. At that time my father, despite his discontent, had a young family of his own. I was not to be a part of that family; so I was adopted by an elderly couple who loved me very much and cared for me as if I was their own child.

In my childhood years, while I realised there was something which was not quite right, I didn't understand the full implications. The turning point came one day when I was coming home from school and friends began to taunt me about who my 'parents' might be. As I say, I knew that my real mother was dead but only then was I taken aside and the whole story revealed to me. In the years that followed, my life became a vicious circle of loneliness and insecurity. I became rebellious and found it difficult to make real friends. My insecurity made me lack the trust that needs to exist between true friends. Insecurity bred loneliness and loneliness, in turn, bred further insecurity. I was in a mess emotionally.

Almost inevitably, my insecurity led me into drugs. I got my first taste of them at the age of fourteen. Drugs, when mixed with drink, give a false sense of security and under their influence I got on better with young people. My inhibitions vanished. But the 'high' too quickly went and it wasn't long before I was looking for more - and another vicious circle would begin. Over those years I worked my way from valium, through cannabis and eventually to heroin. Ultimately the circle ended, as most circles of that type do, with periods in hospital, often up to three months at a time.

By the age of seventeen I was a registered drug addict and was also leading a double life through my involvement with protestant para-militaries. Eventually, in 1982, I was arrested on arms charges and sent to Crumlin Road prison. While I was there, the only woman I had ever known as 'mother', my guardian, died. At this point I hit rock bottom. I had no family, no home, no future and no hope.

When I was released from prison, the whole nasty cycle of drugs and para-militaries began all over again. Like a wanderer, I kept moving from house to house and then from hostel to hostel.

If there is one thing worse than being a homeless junkie, it's being an unemployed, homeless junkie. The depression, due to lack of cash, lack of food and the boredom of each day, with nothing to get out of bed for and nowhere to go, led me to attempt to take my life and thus break the relentless spiral. But I believe now that, even at this point, God was watching over me.

In January 1987, I was again arrested for arms offences and it was while on remand at this time that I began the real search for some meaning to my life, some direction.

Up until this point, God was someone I only thought about in times of trouble and I suppose, when you consider the kind of life I was leading, I should have been thinking quite a lot more about him. So I asked a prison officer for a Bible and began reading from the beginning, in Genesis.

I should say now that, at the time of my suicide attempt, some Christians had brought me face to face with the message of the gospel. I did make a profession of faith then, but like the individual in the parable of the sower, as soon as persecution came I weakened and fell away. However, God is gracious and although I was in a cold and backslidden state he still loved me. Through reading His word again in the prison cell, the Holy Spirit spoke to me in that still, small voice. I was granted the sweet grace of repentance and responded to his call with a simple but earnest, "God help me."

There was no flash of light or voice of thunder, but I felt such a surge of joy and peace and a realisation that indeed my sins were forgiven. I was twenty-two years old. My circumstances hadn't changed but I felt that I had. Christ was again reigning in my life!

Since then, he has provided me with everything I have. A house and all its furnishings; a job as Schools Evangelist with E.Y.M. Ministries, where I'm truly happy working for him; and much more than that, the fulfilment of every desire that I have ever had. I have at last found peace of mind and healing for my sin sick soul.

CHAPTER ONE

RECOLLECTIONS

"CAN A WOMAN FORGET HER SUCKING CHILD, THAT SHE SHOULD NOT HAVE COMPASSION ON THE SON OF HER WOMB. YEA THEY MAY FORGET, YET WILL I NOT FORGET THEE"
ISAIAH 49 v.15.

It was the start of a typical day in Rockland Street, Belfast. My mother called up the stairs for me to get up and I realised that morning had come again. Ignoring her shouts, I lay in bed for a few moments more, wondering what sort of a day I would have.

I was just nine years old and Sarah, whom I looked upon as my mother, was beginning to bug me with all this shouting to get me up for school. I tossed and turned a bit more trying hard to wipe the sleep from my eyes. Then, with another great yawn and a stretch I made the final effort and tumbled out of bed. Still bleary eyed and wearing my pyjamas, I made my way down stairs and tucked into the breakfast which Sarah had prepared.

After breakfast, I washed and dressed and made ready to leave for school. The front door of our house in Rockland Street was partly open and very soon there came the rap that signalled me every morning and the voice that called out, "Are you ready there, Graham."

It was my best mate, Sandy.

With a quick kiss for mum, I was out on the street with Sandy and on the way to school. Sandy and I were in the same class at school and as we strolled along that morning, we chatted away about the usual boys topics - the comics we had read; last night's television and who was the best fighter in our school, Donegal Road Primary.

We arrived just as school commenced and, with lots of the usual pushing and shoving, hurried to get in line.

As we found our places, the playground noises gradually subsided and we waited to be led away by our respective teachers.

I was in P5 and our class had an upstairs room. The brief silence of the playground was soon shattered as boys and girls filed up the staircase, with those behind poking and pinching those in front and the efforts of teachers to enforce law and order proving quite fruitless. As usual, even before lessons for the day began, there were two or three of us brought to the front of the class to be reprimanded.

After suitable chastisement, we were sent back to our seats and only then could our teacher, Mr. Boyd, get on with marking the register. As our names were called out in order we, in turn, chanted out our replies.

"Here Sir!" "Present sir!" "He's not here yet, Sir!" "She's sick, Sir!"

After roll call, "Boydy," as he was known to us, gave the order to get ready for assembly. Very few of us had much interest in things religious so as we lined up there was a lot of complaining under our breaths and a lot of quiet wishing that it would soon be over. As we filed back down the staircase again, on our way to assembly, "Boydy's" voice boomed out, "Keep it quiet there! And stay in single file!"

The assembly hall was a big modern building at the front of the school. Inside it had a fresh, clean smell and a newly waxed floor that gleamed with the morning light that streamed in through the windows.

By the time we arrived, the hall was already half filled with children from the junior section. The noise of sixty or so babbling children was amplified by the echo of the place and it took the headmaster a minute or two to quieten them down before beginning the service.

After the usual greeting of, "Good morning and welcome", the assembly began with morning prayers. One of the P7 pupils read the daily Bible lesson and after this we all joined in the singing of a hymn and the reciting of the Lord's prayer.

"Our Father which art in heaven hallowed be thy name. Thy kingdom come, thy will be done, on earth as it is in Heaven. Give us this day our daily bread and forgive us our trespasses, as we forgive those that trespass against us. And lead us not into temptation but deliver us from evil. For thine is the kingdom and the power and the glory for ever and ever. Amen."

Assembly lasted only a short time but, to us, it seemed like an eternity. Afterwards it was back to classes and the books. The rest of the day at Donegal Road Primary was very much like any other with "Boydy" his usual grumpy self and seizing every opportunity to humiliate anyone who dared to cross his path.

The school had been burned down a few years earlier and when it was modernised, instead of having the usual familiar school bell, a siren was introduced. It was very loud and many a time made us jump in our seats. But when it sounded at the end of each school day it was like music to our young ears.

On the way home from school we chatted and talked, the way boys do, about the events of the day and the run-ins with "Boydy" and things like that.

One day, however, the talk was of a much more serious nature and as it was to turn out, very disturbing for me.

Sammy Brown was another of the lads who lived in our street. He was about a year older than me. On reflection he was probably a lot more worldy wise too - or else he overheard conversation in his own home that he wasn't meant to hear.

Anyway, as we walked home from school on this particular day, Sammy began asking questions about my real mother and who she had been. It was all probably quite innocent and I'm sure he never intended to upset me. However, it all set me thinking and wondering and puzzling, so that by the time I arrived home I was in a really troubled state.

At this stage of my very young life, all I knew was that my real mother was dead and that the woman whom I called 'Mother,' was simply my guardian. I was completely ignorant of everything else.

However, this conversation on the way home from school brought the whole business to a head and filled my mind with all sorts of doubts and fears. I came home that day distressed and crying, and immediately threw a tantrum in front of Sarah, my guardian.

"It's all your fault! It's all your fault!" I shouted. "You didn't want me to have a proper Mum or Dad ... or brothers and sisters! You wanted me to be all on my own!

It took quite a while for Sarah to calm me down. Eventually however, with a lot of hugs and kisses and assurances that she loved me more than life itself and that, as far as she was concerned, I was her own son, she managed to dry my tears and reassure me. Then she promised that, later on that night, she would tell me the full story of my mother, who she was - and where I had come from.

All this was enough to persuade me to go upstairs and change from my school uniform into my old faded jeans. It's a strange thing now and it may seem very insignificant to a lot of people, but as I look back on that day, those jeans, faded and worn as they were, were probably my most treasured possession.

When I came back down stairs again, Sarah, who was a very kind woman really and spoiled me, had a cup of tea ready, just as she had every day when I came in from school.

As the evening wore on and my curiosity heightened I began asking questions about myself and my mother until, eventually, Sarah sat me down and began to recall the past. As she spoke, I began to picture in my mind's eye, the events that must have taken place some eight years before. It all began on the night my mother died.

It was just after midnight on the 13th February 1966 and Sarah had just gone to bed. As she lay there, waiting for sleep to come, her thoughts troubled her. Her daughter Sylvia lay in hospital in a coma.

Sylvia was a diabetic and had been unwell for years. Sarah had constantly nagged her about her diet but Sylvia had rather a sweet tooth and now, sadly, was paying the price for her carelessness. Her blood had clotted, she had lapsed into this coma and now, her life hung in the balance.

Downstairs sat Sarah's husband Sammy and his brother Walter. Sammy was housebound these days because he had lost a leg some years earlier. Before that he had been known as quite a character in the local area and in the pub at the corner of Broadway. But now, a partial cripple, he was almost completely dependent on Sarah and Walter.

Came the early hours of the morning and there was a knock on the front door. Walter went to answer it and when he drew open the door, a policeman stood there. He brought the sad news that Sylvia had passed away without ever regaining consciousness.

Lying upstairs in bed and still troubled by her thoughts, Sarah had heard the knock at the door and then the muffled conversation between Walter and the policeman. She instinctively knew that it spelt bad news. At first she was broken hearted, then hysterical and eventually the doctor had to be called to sedate her.

We lived in a very close knit community and although it was the early hours of the morning, it didn't take long for the neighbours to catch on that something was wrong. They heard the commotion and very quickly gathered round to offer sympathy and support. Amongst them were two of Sarah's oldest friends, Aggie and Mary.

I was only ten months old and because Sarah was in such a troubled state, some of these kind neighbours took me and looked after me for a couple of weeks until things settled down again.

The days following Sylvia's death, leading up to the funeral, were sad and hectic. Walter's two sons-in-law, Frankie and Roy, made all the funeral arrangements. Throughout each day my mother's friends and workmates called to express their sympathy and to offer Sarah whatever help they could.

Most of these people were connected to the bar trade, where Sylvia had been a popular employee. And along with their offers of help, came promises that they would assist Sarah to support and raise the little infant that Sylvia had left behind.

On the morning of the funeral Sarah was outside on the street when a large and expensive car drew up beside her.

A well dressed man stepped out and introduced himself to Sarah. Even before he got out of the car, Sarah had her suspicions as to his identity. Her mind flitted back to a time when Sylvia had described him to her and she knew this stranger was my father.

They stood and talked for a while during which time the man referred to Sylvia and to himself and to how close they had been to each other at one time.

The conversation turned to me and the man explained that, due to his own family commitments, he couldn't get too deeply involved with me. But he did promise to go beyond the regular maintainance payments he was making in order to provide for my upbringing. He also promised to give me employment after I left school.

Then, just as quickly as he had come, he stepped into his big car and drove off down the street and, more or less, out of our lives. But not before again expressing his sympathy to Sarah and promising that he'd be back again in a day or two to see how she was getting on.

As Sarah watched the car move off down the street and disappear around the corner, her thoughts turned again to me.

What twist of fate had brought into this world a little one whom no-one really wanted? What would happen to him, now that his mother had been suddenly taken and his father had a family of his own to take care of? And what would his future hold?

As she turned to go back into the house to prepare for the funeral, a friend whom she hadn't seen for a long time came up to her. Their first reaction was to fling their arms around each other and let the tears flow like rivers.

The emotional strain of the last few days drained away and then, as they moved into the house again, they spoke with fondness of their memories of my mother and recalled the old, happier times, like when she used to go on working holidays to Jersey every summer. Sarah forced a smile and said affectionately, "She used to have my heart broke."

At this point the minister, Rev. Gillespie of Broadway Presbyterian Church, on the Falls Road, arrived. He went directly to Sarah, expressed his sympathy, offered some words of comfort and then began the brief funeral service. It was attended by many friends and relatives all of whom had come to pay their last respects to a beautiful, talented, hard working woman - my mother.

During the service Sarah again began to cry and her crying soon became a wailing. So much so that again the neighbours had to gather around to comfort her.

Just then, the first of the funeral cars arrived and an eerie silence descended on the street. Two men in tall hats and tails, looking very solemn and ghostly, walked into the house. They removed their hats and voiced their sympathy as the minister brought the funeral service to a close. Then, quietly and methodically, they went about their business; pulling the shroud over my mother's face; placing the lid on the coffin and finally, screwing it into place. Everyone present suddenly felt the finality of it all.

The coffin was carried outside and the many floral tributes followed. One or two were carefully placed on top of the coffin and the rest were either put alongside it or placed on top of the hearse.

By the time the funeral cortege moved off, the street had filled with people. Most of them were friends and neighbours. Some were just inquisitive, but all of them wanted to show some sign of respect. Yet none of them knew what to do or say.

Every so often the cortege halted to allow another set of pall bearers to take a 'lift' at the coffin. At last it was placed in the hearse and moved off on its slow and steady journey to my mother's final place of rest.

At the cemetery, the service was brief. Four close members of the family carried my mother's coffin to the side of the open grave where it was reverently lowered into the ground with the words, "Earth to earth, ashes to ashes, dust to dust, in sure and certain hope of the resurrection."

Thus did my mother's short and painful life end and thus was she ushered from this scene of time.

CHAPTER TWO

GOING ASTRAY

*"ALL WE LIKE SHEEP HAVE GONE ASTRAY, WE HAVE
TURNED EVERYONE TO HIS OWN WAY."*
ISAIAH 53 v 6.

As Sarah concluded her story, it brought great sadness to my young, innocent heart and I suppose that even then, I began to realise what a cruel place this world can be.

But at such a tender age, I was not to realise what troubles, and hardships were yet in front of me; nor what the Lord, in his great mercy, was to do for me and through me.

The facts about my mother's life and death, as recounted by Sarah, made me a little more content, at least for a while, but they didn't really change anything.

It was when I started Kelvin Secondary School that my troubles really began. Sarah, who had brought me up from birth and had done so much for me, was now seventy-seven years old and so, understandably, couldn't guide me or control me in the way that a younger person could.

I began hanging around with a crowd of lads who were a few years older and a lot more street-wise than I was. By nature I was very shy and consequently, easily led. It wasn't long before I was playing truant from school, taking strong drink and even dabbling now and then in drugs. It was a short step from this type of foolish behaviour to petty crime. Very soon I was breaking into factories and building sites in the hope of picking up some easy money.

During this time Sarah's health had been deteriorating rapidly. She had cancer and so it was only a matter of time until she would be taken from me forever. Even this didn't have the effect upon me that it should. In fact, it made it easier for me to going further and further down that wrong road. Eventually, Sarah became so weak that she could no longer make her way up and down the stairs, so to make what was left of her troubled life easier for her, a bed was brought down to the front living room. This left the whole of the upstairs of our house open to me.

I had become very interested in rock music and was a keen collector of rock albums. Over the next few months I turned my bedroom into a shrine to rock music and spent most of my free time there, listening to the music and, I suppose, allowing it to mould my mind and my life. My friends used to come and go regularly too, banging doors and tramping up and down the stairs at all hours. All this activity, plus the loud music, was a source of great annoyance to Sarah. In her frail condition she just couldn't cope with it.

It also caused a lot of friction between myself and Sarah's two nieces who used to visit her several times a week. One was called Joan and lived just around the corner from us. The other one, Betty, lived on the other side of town. Both of these ladies had grown up families of their own but they spent a lot of time with Sarah, doing what they could to help and comfort her in her illness. I must say at this point that both Joan and Betty were very good to Sarah and I'd also have to add that they did their very best for me too.

At the same time, I'd have to confess that I was very jealous of Joan's family because it was so happy and complete. Joan and her husband had three sons. I thought

18

those boys were so lucky to have a father to play with them and a mother to love them. I had none of these things and it made me feel very lonely and insecure. However, none of that was Joan's fault. She and her family are lovely people.

Growing up in the Donegal Road area, 'The village,' as it's known locally, meant coming under very strong paramilitary influences. In a working class neighbourhood like that, it was almost every young lad's dream to grow up to be, 'one of the boys.' It's hardly surprising then, that I too was to fall into that same trap at a very tender age. In fact I was just fifteen when I first got involved.

It came about, very simply, through my association with a lad I had grown up with. He was a few years older than me and had been recruited by the local Ulster Defence Association, (U.D.A.). At seventeen he was already heavily involved in the organisation and one day he asked me to do a favour for them. I did it and one small thing led to another and then another, so that by the time I was sixteen, I had been sworn in as a fully pledged member of the UDA.

Shortly after this, five of us were sent out on a particular mission and happened to be caught by the police, redhanded. Very soon I had my first experience of Castlereagh holding centre and shortly after, of Crumlin Road prison. It resulted in a week of my life that I will never forget.

The first time I stepped into that cell I tried to act like a hard man. I tried to show the police that really I couldn't care less about what I had done and what might happen to me. But in reality I was scared out of my wits. The thought of being locked up for months, maybe even years, brought terror to my young heart. I remember the tremendous sense of loneliness that came over me when that cell door clanged behind me, closing me in and taking away my liberty. The seriousness of the situation hit me like a sledge hammer and the minutes and hours that followed, crawling in at a snail's pace, gave me plenty of time to reflect on the hopelessness of my position.

Eventually, I was charged with possession of a firearm and sent to prison on remand until the case could be brought before the courts. However, because it was my first terrorist offence I suppose, I was released on bail after a few days. How good it felt to be out again and breathing the good fresh air of home.

Sarah's health had been deteriorating to such an extent that she had been taken into hospital. I used to visit her every day, sometimes twice a day when I could. I can remember so clearly the last time I went to see her - the last time I saw her alive.

It was on the morning of the day when I had to go back to the court to be re-remanded pending my trial. I knew I would have to go back to prison to await trial and, as I stood there by Sarah's bedside, somehow I knew this would be the last time I would see her in this world. It was clear that she wouldn't last much longer so, as I squeezed her hand that morning and whispered my goodbye, there were great big tears in my eyes.

As I walked away, I knew I had said my last farewell to the one lady in this world who had shown me kindness and love. She had done her very best for me. Now she could do no more. Sarah died nine days later in her hospital bed. I was in "A" wing of Crumlin Road prison.

CHAPTER THREE

ON THE WAY TO JAIL

"WHATSOEVER A MAN SOWETH THAT SHALL HE ALSO REAP."
GALATIANS 6 v 7.

The big police man opened the door and shouted to us in between talking to his mate, "Let's have you lads!"

After my first spell in jail life had gone from bad to worse. Eventually I had fallen out with the UDA and moved up to live in the Ballysillan area of north Belfast, where I joined the Ulster Volunteer Force, (UVF.) The UVF was a much more active organisation and before I knew it, I was once again involved in serious crime, this time with a loaded gun. And that's how I had landed myself in this present rather sticky mess.

In one heaving mass we got to our feet and headed for the door which the 'cop' held open.

He ushered us through, one at a time, to another officer who hand-cuffed us and pointed us toward a long landing. At the end of the landing there were more police officers. In fact they were everywhere.

They checked our names and photographs; confirmed our identities; checked the handcuffs again and then led us outside to a courtyard.

"It's about time!" one of the fellows remarked, doing his best to be cheeky. He was answered with an equally sarcastic remark from one of the policemen and a caution to, "stop girnin'."

Out in the courtyard, the vans which would take us to Crumlin Road prison were parked. They were big, dark blue personnel carriers which we nicknamed 'paddy waggons', or 'horse boxes', and they were specially designed and fitted out for carrying prisoners.

In the back of them were cells or cubicles; hospital clean on the outside but stinking inside. Each cubicle was about three feet square and about six feet high with a built in seat fastened to the wall.

In summer the seat was roasting hot and in winter freezing cold. Because of this I usually stood up on my journeys in the 'paddy waggon,' but at a bit of a slant or with my head hung low; squeezing in my six foot two height. How I longed to be a couple of inches shorter on those journeys. But I suppose the vans weren't built exactly for comfort.

The journey from Chichester Street Magistrates Court seemed to be taking longer than usual. I say longer than usual because at this stage I had been in and out of jail like a yo-yo and so had taken this trip several times before.

There were no windows in the van so I had no way of knowing where I was, except that, every now and then, the van came to a stop. Every time it did so, I wondered if this would be its arrival at the prison. Eventually however, it did and I heard the clang of the outer prison gate slamming behind us. The van's engine was shut off and then I could hear the sounds of prison officer's voices calling out and giving the all clear to open the inner gate. Then the sound of an air compressor as the steel wall in front of us slid open automatically giving us access to the prison courtyard. At last we had arrived at Belfast's Crumlin Road prison.

For a short time, no-one came near us and I began to get very impatient, anxiously wanting to get the formalities of reception to prison over with. Eventually, there was a movement at the back of the van as the main door swung open and the welcome breath of fresh air came wafting in. Next the jangle of keys as the cubicle doors were unlocked and each prisoner was led out.

At last it was my turn. I had been sitting for a while but at the first sign of the cubicle door being opened I was on my feet and looking forward to stretching my legs again. How I detested riding in that prison van. It was like a sardine can. In fact, I thought sardines had a lot more room than we did.

Once out of the van we were ushered into a small corridor. It had once been white but over the years had become grubby and dismal. It was very narrow and along one side of it there were little openings which looked like windows, except that instead of glass they had doors which could be opened from the office behind them.

We all stood in a row facing one of these little doors. Above my head there were three spotlights. Two of them pointed at the wall behind me and the other down at the ground in front of my feet.

Suddenly one of the little doors opened and a voice bellowed out at me, "Get off the wall!"

I moved over to the window where an officer was beckoning me with a wave of his hand and then came the questions. "What are you in for?" "Possession," I answered. "Have you been here before?" "Aye, I'm never out." I was trying to play the hard man. "What were you in for before?" "Same thing. They'll throw away the key. I'll get double figures this time."

Double figures means a jail sentence of more than nine years.

After taking note of all the details, like my full name, address, next of kin and doctor's name, the prison officer told me to go back over against the wall while he called forward someone else. At the same time he gave me my prison number which was in the four hundreds. That meant there had been more than four hundred men sentenced in that month. I remember reflecting that that was quite a staggering figure for a place as small as Northern Ireland, with a population of just over a million and a half.

Some of these would be 'fine' men; people who had refused to or who couldn't pay their fines. They would just do a day or two. Some would be young offenders; on their way to a Young Offenders Centre. Some would be long term men; en route to the Maze or Magilligan. The remainder were people like myself; 'doing their time', in Crumlin Road.

I stood there for a few moments mulling these thoughts over in my head and then an officer wearing a long blue coat, like an overall, confronted me. He had an instamatic camera slung around his neck. Reaching above my head he flicked a switch which turned on the spotlights, flooding the area where I stood with light.

The officer thrust a board into my hands and ordered me to hold it against my chest while he took a picture. On the board were my name, date of birth and prison number.

After this, I was led through the grill on my right into a larger open area where there were lots more of these officers wearing blue coats over their uniforms. No sooner had the grill clanged shut behind me than the order was barked out for me to strip.

"Get your clothes off and put that around you!"

One of the orderlies had given me what looked like a pillow case which had been ripped along the seams. But when I attempted to wrap it round me it was too small, so I had no option but to hold it in front of me in an effort to retain some semblance of modesty. I felt really silly and embarrassed. On reflection, I must have looked a right eejit standing there naked, except for a pillow case that felt no bigger than a hanky.

"Stand up on the scales. Stand up straight with your hands by your sides."

The officer brought a stick, which was fastened to a ruler, down on my head. "Six foot one and a half and thirteen and a half stone." He called out my height and weight to another officer who marked it down for the prison records.

Finally, after taking note of my tattoos, scars and other distinguishing marks, I was sent off to have a shower; compulsory for all new inmates.

I looked forward to this with some relish for it had been a long day. All the hassle of courts, police cars and paddy waggons had taken their toll and I was now very tired. A shower would refresh me, or so I thought. As it happened, the water was so hot it literally almost took the skin off me.

The basement cells were the same as they had always been in my memory. Nothing had changed, not even the dismal cream colour of those drab walls. The inmates hadn't changed much either. There were the same old faces of the orderlys and some of the prisoners seemed to have been there for ever.

The truth was that they were all very much like myself. Most of them were men who had been in and out of prison several times. They would be serving short sentences, never more than eighteen months at a stretch and all of them for minor crimes like shoplifting, petty theft or being drunk and disorderly.

There was one fellow there who had been in prison every year for the past twenty years and he loved it. He had no responsibilities there. No rent to pay, none of the pressures of the outside world and all his food provided. He was actually happier in jail.

There were a lot of men like that in Crumlin Road. Quite a few were 'lifers,' or long term men, doing more than four years. Because of family breakdowns, inferiority complexes or the jail routine, to which they were now accustomed, they had become institutionalised and no longer had any desire to be out of jail; at least not for very long. "God forbid that I would ever get to that stage," I thought.

The cell they put me in was half way up the right hand side of the landing. It had two bunks in it, a double and a single. The moment I stepped into it the cell door slammed behind me and the key rattled in the lock - a final solemn reminder that I was now a prisoner.

After looking around the drab cell, I sat down on the edge of one of the bunks and began to ponder who my cells mates would be. I wasn't left alone for too long. The cell door opened again and a young lad who must have been about six foot six in height came in, crouching a little to get in through the six foot door opening.

"What about you," he said. "Dead on," I replied. "Are you here long?" "No mate, I'm only in,"

The conversation continued in this vein for a while until the door opened again and the third member of our trio walked in.

He was about my height and wearing glasses. He passed a comment about how tiny the cell was and then told us he had never been in before.

"Don't worry about it," says I, "you'll soon get used to it."

There followed further brief introductions and some small talk about what each of us was in for. These included our exaggerated side of the story and the bravery we had shown when questioned by the police. We more or less said, "Boy we really showed them who was boss." It seemed strange to me that we had all made statements admitting our guilt and now we all seemed so brave.

After about half an hour the call came for tea, and with our big plastic mugs, which held more than a pint, we sallied forth to the meal trolley.

I've never tasted crude oil but I imagine it couldn't be any worse than the margarine we were given to spread on our bread. To accompany the bread there were soggy fish cakes and tinned peas, plus the pint mug of liquid tar that the prison officers had the audacity to call tea. It's amazing how quickly your appetite can go when faced with such a diet.

I couldn't help smiling at one of my cell mates, the one who hadn't been in before. On the meals trolley he spotted a dixie full of what he assumed to be sugar and proceeded to help himself. The orderlys, who enjoy a laugh at the expense of prisoners, did nothing to correct his notion and before anyone else could intervene he had loaded his tea with two large spoonsful of coarse cooking salt. "You have an awful lot to learn," I thought, "and like me, you'll probably have to learn it the hard way."

We brought the meals back to the cell and after a few sarcastic comments about them, tucked in. There wasn't really any option.

The rest of the evening was spent in small talk till, at eleven o'clock, the lights went out, leaving us in the dark with each other ... and our thoughts.

There was a lot of tossing and turning in the rather cramped bunks and as is often the case at times like this, sleep was a long time in coming. After a while I gave up the prospect and reached to the floor for my snout tin.

"Anybody want a roll up?"

One of the cell mates took a cigarette but the other politely refused, thanking me anyway. Every draw on the cigarette lit up the cell with a faint glow and I couldn't help noticing the worried faces of my two companions. What thoughts went through their minds?

Perhaps, like me, they were anxious to know if there were any old enemies in the prison. The only thing worse than doing time is doing it with someone you either hate the sight of or fear so much that it keeps you awake at night. In circumstances like that prison can be a very small place.

I was thinking about which wing I would be placed in, who the commander would be and what excuse I could think up for having made a statement to the police while in Castlereagh. Boy, that would be a tricky one to get out of. They hated anyone making statements, and to make matters even worse I had picked the wrong solicitor to represent me. All this would have to be explained and I had no idea where to begin.

I was also thinking about the political climate in the jail. Had there been any trouble? Had the Provos (Provisional I.R.A.) caused any hassle? Were there any protests against the 'screws,' as we called the prison officers. I wondered, too, about the other men in the prison. How many U.V.F. and U.D.A. men would there be? Would they be at peace with one another or would there still be the usual friction sparked off either by personality clashes, or power struggles?

Of course, when all this in-fighting was going, on the Provos sat back and had a good laugh at it all. All these thoughts flooded my mind and added to the frustration of not being able to sleep. However, eventually, sleep did come.

Next morning we were brought out to be photographed again and finger-printed. Then there was the doctor, the welfare officer and the chaplain to see. There was also a bed back to make up and a cell to clean. It looked liked being a very busy morning.

"Right young Lawther, away and see the Vicar, kid!"

The officer opened the cell door and I stepped out and walked down the landing, keeping close to the wall and falling in at the back of the queue. Three of us lined up outside the welfare office where we would meet the minister who was Presbyterian.

"Come in young fellow, sit yourself down there."

This is how I was introduced to the man who was to become not only a brother in the Lord but also a very dear friend. In fact, he still remains a close friend to this day.

The Reverend Jackson Buick was the Presbyterian chaplain for the prison - a jolly wee man about five foot two, with a bald head and a big smile. He was well on in years, at least sixty I thought, but by the look of him he had a good chance of outliving us all.

He spoke kindly to me in his husky voice, enquiring after my welfare and promising to give me any help he could.

At that time my thoughts were far from God. I could see no further than the rat race I was caught up in and had little time for anyone else. Consequently, our meeting that morning was a brief one. Thank God there were more to come. Since then I have cherished his advice and have been greatly influenced by him to search for holiness and trust only in the Lord.

Back in my cell, my thoughts still troubled me. It was now just after lunch time lock up and I had been in prison since the day before, Friday.

Even though I had been in custody since the previous Tuesday I still hadn't been asked to give an explanation for my arrest and this troubled me. I sat there in the cell quietly contemplating what I would say to my commander. Every last detail would have to be given and I would have to be sure to forget nothing; nor to add anything that I might later accidentally contradict.

About a dozen of us lined up with our belongings waiting to hear which wing we would be sent to. I knew I'd be sent to either 'A' or 'C', the two paramilitary wings.

There was silence as we waited for our names to be called, a silence broken only by the intermittent bark of the officer's voice as he called out first the surname and then the wing. Somewhere in the middle of it all I heard my name and the announcement that I was going to 'A' wing.

This was the best that I could have expected. I was familiar with 'A' wing. It was the biggest and cleanest wing and most of the officers were sound men. Mind you the odd one seemed to think of himself as a little Hitler. But you get that type of person everywhere, not just in prisons.

Oh yes, 'A' wing would be the best place to be in. The only thing that worried me was the fact that it housed some of the toughest paramilitaries, men who were top security risks and needed constant surveillance. Some of them I genuinely feared because of their bad reputation for violence outside the prison. But I would just have to get over this hurdle when I came to it. Not much point in worrying now.

On the way up the stairs and through all the different security grills and doors I wondered who the commander might be. Would I know him? And for that matter, would he know me? I remembered an incident a few months back when five lads from Ballysillan were jailed for arms offences. Could it be one of them?

What seemed like an eternity passed and then the door swung open, allowing those of us who were bound for 'A' wing to pass through and, once again, line up. I was assigned to 'A-3' and told to go up and see Mr. Rea.

Mr. Rea was very friendly at first, laughing and joking with me as he took particulars of my name, date of birth, name of my doctor, and so on. But then his mood changed and he became quite serious.

"What are you in for?" "Possession," I replied. " A r e you a hood or a paramilitary," he enquired. "A paramilitary." "What - U.V.F?" he asked.

There was a cold silence as I searched for the right words. They wouldn't come. I hadn't been expecting that question so it came very much as a shock to me. I guess my silence looked like an acknowledgment of guilt.

At this point Mr. Rea told me the name of the U.V.F. commander in the jail. The commander was well known in the district where I lived but although I had heard of him, I had never actually met him. As I stood there, I just wondered if he knew me.

Mr. Rea broke into my thoughts with instructions as to how he liked the cell block to be kept.

"Keep yourself clean and your cell clean," he said. "As if I need you to tell me that," I thought. I had been in and out of prison like a yo-yo and didn't need him to educate me.

"Mind your own business and nobody will hassle you," he continued. "Any requests, seven thirty A.M. at your door, dressed and standing up straight. Understood?"

"Aye," I said, and at that, he told me what cell I would be in. "Away and throw your gear in and go on outside. The prods are on A.S.O."

Chapter Four

MEETING THE COMMANDER

"The fear of man bringeth a snare."
Proverbs 29 v 25.

The prison canteen was much smaller than I had expected; about half the size. As well as the usual dining tables and chairs, there was an old, worn out pool table and a home made table-tennis table.

On one wall there was a dart board and four darts and in the corner, a television set which was controlled by the prison officer who sat outside in the security box.

The first thing that struck me about the place was how untidy and dirty it was. The drab, off-white walls were long overdue for a lick of fresh paint and the dull red floor obviously hadn't known either polish or elbow grease for years. It certainly wasn't what I expected in the ultra clean prison system I was used to.

Apparently, the reason for this was that the paramilitaries themselves had chosen the cleaning orderlies and on this occasion hadn't done so very well.

The first person I spoke to was a lad from Bangor. He was a hood who, like the rest of us, thought he was of some importance and claimed to be a top man in the Red Hand

Commandos, another protestant para-military group. He had a pointy face and in certain respects his features resembled those of a horse. It's not surprising, then, that they nicknamed him 'horsey head.'

When I first met him he was standing with a fellow from Lisburn, nicknamed 'Golfball.' Golfball and another young lad had been charged with beating a Catholic to death with a pool cue.

Both of these lads were mates, from the same housing estate in Lisburn. Both were members of the same U.D.A. division and now both were on remand, charged with the same offence. There was one other thing common to them. Both vehemently denied the charges.

"What are you in for?" were horsey head's first words to me when he called me over. By this time I was sick of that question. It was the first thing everybody said when they met you and it became very tiresome, like a cracked gramophone record.

"Possession of a firearm with intent to endanger life," was my stock answer. I saw no need to change it now. But then came the next question.

"Are you in anything?" "I want to see the U.V.F. commander," was my stern reply.

Horsey head informed me that the commander was busy just now but that he would see me shortly and then enquired if I was from Ballysillan.

When I replied in the affirmative he said, "Oh, you'll know him then. He's from your neck of the woods."

As soon as he told me the commander's name I realised that this was the man I had heard about. He was indeed a commander in Ballysillan and had a reputation for being a first class operator. He was also very popular within the organisation, especially with the high ranking officers and was a personal friend of the North Belfast Brigadier, who had recently been murdered by an I.R.A. hit squad.

The commander recognised me immediately and referred to me as the painter. That was because I had once painted a UVF mural on a gable wall in Ballysillan. He had seen me at it and remembered me from there.

Our conversation wasn't nearly as bad as I had expected. In fact the man was quite friendly and very easy to get along with.

First he asked me a few questions about my interview in the police barracks and then enquired about the gun I was caught with. It was a point two five Colt which he said was useless because it was impossible to get any ammunition for it.

"Useless or not," I thought, "I had been caught with it ... loaded."

I went on to explain how I thought I had been caught, telling him some truth and making up the rest of it as I went along.

I put most of the blame on a guy who had fled to England after having been shot in both legs outside the loyalist club one Sunday night in what the U.V.F. called a punishment shooting. His crime? Anti-social behaviour.

It suited me well to blame this fellow because he wasn't there to defend himself. And even if he had been there, nobody would have believed him. After the punishment shooting he had lost all credibility.

The conversation ended with the commander asking me if I had everything I needed. Even though I said I was well enough supplied with with everything, including tobacco, he insisted on giving me some more.

"Follow me down to my cell after lock up and I'll sort you out," he said.

We talked for a while longer and quickly became quite friendly, laughing, joking and carrying on at a great rate.

"You'll be about fifty when they let you out," he said.
"At least I'll get out. You've no hope," I retorted.

Before we knew it, it was seven o'clock and lock up time was being called. Lock up is the term used in prison to indicate that association between prisoners is over and it's time for men to go back to their own cells.

The paramilitaries call their own lock up, or if you like, give the order for their men to go back to their cells. They like to give the impression that they are in control of their own affairs, so the order to go back to the cells usually comes only after the prison officers have called for it several times.

On the way back to the cells the noise was incredible, with the prisoners shouting to each other and the officers running about wildly and also shouting in an effort to get everybody back into the cells so they could go home.

I walked back to my cell in the company of the commander; to collect the stuff he had for me. On the way, he told me about the parade which was to be held the next day.

"You have to put your shoes on to come into the yard! Have you ever been to a parade before?" "Aye, Aye," says I, "I've been to parades before," trying to pretend that I'd been to more parades than I could remember. "You'll know the score then," he said.

As soon as we got to his cell he asked the prison officer to hold on a minute while he put together a parcel for me. It all happened so quickly that I never saw what he put in the bag. Then it was a quick 'good-night' and back to my own cell.

The cell itself was all right but there was another fellow in it and I found him very hard to get along with. He was very quiet and didn't want to do much talking, so he wasn't the best of company for me.

To be quite truthful about it, I was glad to see him getting bail for it's far better doing time on your own, when you can do your own thing, than to be stuck with somebody whom you're always afraid of offending.

For instance, you can imagine the problems that arise when you want go to sleep and your cell mate wants to listen to the radio. As well as that, if one person in the cell is in bad form or depressed, it has a knock on effect on the rest of the men there. So, all in all, it's far better to be on your own.

When I got back to the cell, the first thing I did was to open he parcel the UVF commander had given me. I was truly amazed. There was everything in it that I could possibly have needed - teabags, sugar, coffee, biscuits, even hankies! And, of course, snout and fag papers.

I felt a lot better now. The initial introduction to the commander had gone better than expected and it was now only a matter of taking it a day at a time and crossing each bridge as I came to it.

I fell asleep that night thinking of the parade next day. Had it changed much since the last time I had been to one? Would I make a fool of myself? When everyone else was making a right turn would I make a left? "Oh boy", I thought, "if I make a mess of this I'll never hear the end of it."

The next day started with the usual relaxed atmosphere of every Sunday morning. First, there came the breakfast call and then the cleaning out of our cells. After this, it was down to the wash house to spruce up, or if you were lucky, have a shower.

Later the call came for the Roman Catholics to attend Mass. This was known to us simply as R.C. worship and from our cells we could hear them being called. Shortly after, there was the shuffling of feet and the babble of voices as they made their way along to the service.

Once they were all safely settled in their place of worship we were allowed out to the exercise yard.

We all wore coats and shoes for the parade and as we went out we were searched. Waiting in line to go through the security check I couldn't help thinking again about the parade.

But as I looked around me, it seemed I was the only one who felt like this. All the others were laughing and joking. They were probably well used to it by now. Still, there would be no-one happier than me when it was all over.

The exercise yard in 'A' wing was the largest in the prison, about the size of a football pitch. The walls around it were about twenty feet high and they had rows of razor wire along the top of them.

Razor wire is similar to barbed wire except that instead of the familiar spikes or barbs, it has little pieces of razor blade interwoven into the wire. Just a simple mistake there and you would need stitches in the wounds.

At either end of the exercise yard there was a security box which was manned at all times. At strategic positions around the walls there were security cameras which could be remotely controlled. Not a thing could be done in that yard without the authorities being aware of it.

And sometimes we wondered if they could hear us as well. We wouldn't have been surprised if there had been little microphones hidden in the walls too. Every word we spoke was in the very lowest of tones and quite often we reminded each other of the old saying, "walls have ears."

By the time I arrived in the yard it a was hive of activity. There was a sort of football match going on at one end with four or five fellows kicking a ball about between them. Here and there around the yard small groups of men were huddled together, chatting or debating one topic or another. Others preferred to make use of the time and the fresh air to limber up or stretch their legs and spent the time walking round and round the perimeter wall. Some were even ambitious enough to jog and by the time lock-up was called could put in over a hundred laps of the yard, accounting they claimed, for about seven and a half miles.

I had only been there for about fifteen minutes when one of the fellas called out at the top of his voice, "Right lads, fall in."

This was the wing's UDA commander. He was a big, well made fella from Highfield, another area of Belfast, and he had a voice like a regimental sergeant major.

Everyone headed for the wall and began to line up. There was a lot of jostling about as the men tried to find their correct places, tallest to the right, shortest to the left. Eventually the lines were formed and the whole column marched out in threes, until the forty-five of us had formed the parade square of three rows of fifteen in the centre of the yard. I was put in the middle somewhere, so that if I blundered it could be easily covered up.

There followed an uneasy silence for about fifteen seconds.

I was so nervous that my heart was racing. I was so afraid of getting the timing wrong and making myself look a right fool. I felt as if every eye was on me and the whole parade depended on me getting it right.

From where I stood ages seemed to go by before the guy at the back giving the orders shouted, "parade shun!" After that the commands came fast and furious with right turns, left turns, right dress, eyes front and finally, "stand at ease!" The parade concluded with a two minute silence, in memory, I suppose, of loyalists who had been killed. Finally, we were dismissed.

The whole parade, which I had spent half the previous night worrying about, lasted no more than about six minutes.

That worry had been brought on by the stories I had heard from other so called veterans of the organisation. These were men who had been in jail before me and had painted a very frightening picture of UVF discipline in prison. Indeed, both sets of paramilitaries were renowned for their peculiar sense of justice and their punishment of offenders. This was often manifested in the verdicts of their kangaroo courts.

One particular case of this type immediately springs to mind.

A young lad was brought in and accused of beating up and robbing an old age pensioner. In due course he was brought before the paramilitary court. It seems that the prison officers were in on the thing too, because they handed him over to his unofficial judge and jury.

The terms 'judge' and 'jury' are somewhat inappropriate because, even before the young lad arrived in their presence, the decision had been taken to punish him for behaviour unacceptable to society.

About sixty prisoners formed a circle around the young fellow and, when the signal was given, a number of them moved in.

These self appointed administrators of justice punched and kicked their victim for several minutes until the order was given to disperse. When they withdrew he was a sorry sight, but fortunately, not seriously injured.

The UVF looked upon themselves as soldiers and always stressed this point whenever possible. However, the ones who adopted this attitude were usually little jumped-up commanders who were on a personal ego trip and very often only in the organisation as a means of lining their own pockets.

However, as well as these self appointed dictators there were also, from time to time, genuine men who were prepared to 'muck in' with the rest of the boys. On this occasion we seemed to be fortunate enough to get a man like this. He was one of the fairest commanders the loyalist paramilitaries had seen for years.

Exercise was followed by Sunday lunch and by this time I couldn't wait to get at it. I was starving!

Sunday was the best day of the week for food in the prison. It seemed that they really went out of their way to provide a first class meal.

There were two types of potatoes - mash or roast; fresh vegetables and either chicken, steak or roast beef. And to top it all - lashings of gravy. It really was great packing and I enjoyed every mouthful.

There was dessert on Sundays too and sometimes this caused problems. Some of the men were too full after what went before and decided to give the dessert a pass. This led to arguments as to who would have the extra portions. However, the commander usually stepped in with the ideal solution to the problem. He ate it himself!

CHAPTER FIVE

THE UNEXPECTED VISIT

"THEREFORE SNARES ARE AROUND ABOUT THEE AND
SUDDEN FEAR TROUBLETH THEE."
JOB 22 v 10.

The next few weeks in Crumlin Road jail seemed to fly in. There were new faces every day as more and more loyalists were remanded on terrorist offences. During one period of about three days, five or six UVF men came in together.

Meanwhile the UDA members were giving those of us who were in the UVF a lot of stick about how easy it was for the police to catch us. Their superior attitude didn't seem to make a lot of sense to me. After all, if they were so good at getting away, why were they in prison along with us?

However, in jail men behave in a very odd manner and they have a completely different code of conduct to the one they follow outside. In prison there's an unwritten rule that the last man in is the least important. That means that those who are in longer feel superior to the others. Actually, common sense would seem to say that those in first are the bigger fools, they got caught first! But such is man's pride that even in his failures he wants to be reckoned best at it.

Now what I'm going to say next may seem very selfish I know, but at the time I wasn't too sorry to see a few UVF men being caught. It took the heat away from me and I was very glad not to be last man in for too long.

One particular day of the second week I was in prison, stands out clearly in my mind, even now. It was the day I received two unexpected visitors.

When the prison officer first called me for the visit I was so surprised that I asked who had come to see me. Remember, I was an orphan so the last thing I expected was a visit from anyone.

The officer gave me the names of two high ranking UVF men. One of them I knew personally. The other only by name. As soon as I heard their names I was frightened. In fact I was terrified. These men would be looking for answers. Answers that perhaps I couldn't provide.

It's a long walk from the prison cell to the visiting area and the whole way down I remained silent and apparently calm. But inside my heart was pounding and my brain was in a turmoil as I rehearsed, over and over again, the answers I would give to the questions I expected them to ask. Going through the search box the prison officer had to ask me my number twice, so far away were my thoughts.

What would I tell them about Castlereagh holding centre? What questions had the police asked me and what names had they mentioned during the three days I had been there?

The officer at the desk gave me a cubicle number and told me to go and sit at it. In the cubicle there was a table with a chair at one end and two at the other. I sat down on the single chair and waited for my visitors to arrive.

"What about ya," they said as they sat down. "Are you enjoying yourself."

"Aye, it's great," I replied with a hint of sarcasm.

The man that I knew personally spoke to me again, very seriously. "What happened?" he asked.

44

"All right," says I, "I'll tell you the whole story. They caught me with that wee gun and all them rounds of ammo."

"Where did they get you," he continued.

"Just off Manor street ... in that bird's house. That other fella touted on me."

I then proceeded to heap the blame on the chap who had been shot outside the loyalist club and was now in England. I explained how the cops had raided the house at five-thirty in the morning and had found the gun and the ammunition in a lunch box under the bed.

"Castlereagh hasn't changed much, has it?" I said.

"That place will never change," he replied and then went on to ask what the police had questioned me about. I spent the next ten minutes telling him all that had happened and reciting the names of the various people the police had asked me about.

I must add here that the Castlereagh holding centre is, in my opinion, the pits. It was the worst place on earth as far as I was concerned and I really hated it. I was always weak and could never stand the pressure of the interrogation they subjected men to. I used to envy the fellas who could stay in there for seven days and come back out without having batted an eyelid.

On two out of the three occasions I had been held there I ended up making a statement to the police and then spent the rest of the time worrying how I would explain what I had done to the paramilitaries. They don't take kindly to men who break under pressure, no matter how severe it is. On the other hand, whilst there are many stories of men being physically abused while in Castlereagh, I never received any such treatment.

There was one occasion, however, when I did have a rough time from a policeman. I was being interviewed by a big cop in Donegall Pass barracks and in the middle of the questioning he suddenly stopped. Slowly removing his coat and then his watch he came up behind me and grabbed my shirt pulling it down my back until the front top button dug into my Adam's apple, nearly throttling me. Thank God that's as far as he went.

The cells in Castlereagh are not at all like the ones in prison. When I was there they stuck me in a little cubicle with no windows. The single electric light bulb burned all night long, being dimmed only from about midnight till seven in the morning. It's nearly impossible to sleep in conditions like that but I suppose, it's just another part of the mental torture they put you through.

Everything in the cells is chained to the floor. That's in case you get any ideas about having a go at the cops and fancy using some part of the furniture as a weapon.

There's a springless, steel bed with a rubber mattress and paper sheets, just in case the pressure gets too much for you and you want to hang yourself. One fellow, a provo, did just that in the early seventies.

The worst thing about the place was the food. I hated it. Everything was swimming in grease and was served on polystyrene plates which squeaked horribly every time the plastic knife touched them.

In Castlereagh the policemen took it in turns to interview suspects for about two hours at a time. Then to give them a break and, I suppose, keep them fresh and the suspect under pressure, two others took over so that you were faced with a constant barrage of questions in the hope that you would finally crack under the pressure and tell them whatever they wanted to know. At one stage I was being questioned about everything from theft to murder. Thank the Lord I knew nothing about most of these things so couldn't tell them anything.

After relating all this to my two high ranking UVF visitors I had to sit and listen to them harangue me for being so stupid as to get caught and how I could have got away if

I had been clever enough. However, before they left they assured me that the UVF would look after me while I was in prison and they asked me if there was anything I needed. I was afraid to sound greedy and so replied very cautiously, "I could be doing with a radio."

The one who was known to me personally promised that I'd get a radio before very long and added that I'd also be getting the jeans and training shoes that the other UVF prisoners had received at Christmas time.

"Do you have anyone to visit you?" he asked. I replied that, since I had no family of my own and all my mates were working, there was little chance of me having anyone to come and see me. "Well," he said, "I'll make sure that some of the boys come up to see you from time to time. Just send the passes out to my house and I'll take care of it."

With that, the prison officer came up and set the visiting pass on the table indicating that it was time for my two friends to leave. Slowly they got to their feet and left with a friendly, "Cheerio."

As I walked back to my cell I offered a silent prayer of thanks that the visit had gone so well. It hadn't been half as bad as I'd expected and the two men had turned out to be quite friendly.

One of the prison officers in the search box passed a comment to me as I went through.

"The last time I saw those two guys they were sitting on the other side of the table!"

They were former prisoners and had been in as a result of the supergrass system of the late seventies. The evidence of William "Budgie" Allen and Joe Bennett had seen them charged with serious crime but they were acquitted because of insufficient evidence.

Also, on the way back to my cell I bumped into the UVF commander. He was very interested in my two visitors and wanted to hear the whole story.

47

"Come and see me after lock up," he said, " and tell me all about it." I promised him I would.

The lock up time is only two and a half hours but it seemed to drag in that afternoon. When it was over I immediately hurried down the stairs to look for the commander and give him the news about my two important visitors.

When I think back on it, it seems quite comical, even a bit ridiculous. What was the hurry? The news would keep. Neither he nor I would be going anywhere for quite a while.

Maybe it was the fact that he was the UVF commander in the prison that gave it that sense of urgency. Whatever the reason I was behaving, for all the world, like a child that had heard gossip and was running home to tell all to its mother.

The commander was walking around the exercise yard alone when I got there. When he saw me coming he turned towards me and walked my way.

"Well .. what did he say?" The commander went straight to the point. "He was asking about you and he wants you to send him out a pass so that he can come and visit you."

"Aye .. it's a long time since I've had him up to see me. But what else did he say? Did he ask you about getting lifted and so on?"

"He told me I was a right eejit and said I was daft for having the gun under my bed. I suppose he was right!"

I then went on to tell him the whole story of the visit. The questions they asked about my time in Castlereagh. The answers I gave and how they promised to look after me while I was in prison.

"Oh aye .. they'll look after you all right," he said. "But sure why wouldn't they? Aren't you in here for helping them? I think it's £7.00 a week you get if you're single and £12.00 if you're married. Not a lot, is it, for being stuck in here."

I said I'd be glad of it. It would get me snout ... and batteries for that radio they had promised me.

"Oh they're getting you a radio, are they? It'll take a couple of weeks to get that through security ... and by the time they doctor it you'll be lucky if you can get as much as a squeak out of it."

"We'll see," I thought and went back to my cell.

CHAPTER SIX

WHY DID IT HAVE TO HAPPEN TO ME?

"YE SHALL NOT AFFLICT ANY WIDOW OR FATHERLESS CHILD."
EXODUS 22 v 22.

Not having a family, and therefore, no one to visit me in prison, was proving to be rather a hard trial. Despite their promises, the UVF had let me down. They only came to see me now and again, when it suited them, although the money, £7.00 a week, always arrived. It was left in every Friday by a friend's wife.

But the one thing I missed most of all was someone to come and have a chat with me .. someone to care. That half hour or so every week is the thing that most prisoners look forward to. It wasn't so with me and I felt deeply hurt about it.

Alone in the prison and, apparently, forsaken I began to think about my past. I had one of the wealthiest father's in the country and yet he didn't care. He didn't want anything to do with me. I was just an embarrassment to him; a constant reminder of his unfaithfulness to his wife and of a very foolish and expensive mistake. Now here was I, his son, stuck in a miserable prison cell. No family! No home! No future! But worse than that ... no-one who cared.

My father had just been a big windbag. A man full of broken promises and false hopes.

When I was a child, he had promised there would be job for me when I left school - but there had never been a job. He had promised there would be a car for me when I could drive - but there was never a mention of it since. And the hardest thing of all for me to accept was the fact that he didn't love me, especially now when nobody else cared and I needed it most.

Oh there had been occasions when he had given me a few pounds .. mostly at Christmas time and birthdays. But it was only when I contacted him and he felt obliged to give me something to keep me from pestering him.

I could never remember him having a conversation with me or showing any genuine interest in my well being. That's the way he had always been and the years of my growing up hadn't changed him, or if they had, it had only been for the worse.

Even now it's very difficult for me to tell you anything about my father, I know so little about him. I have never known a father's love to protect me ... or his discipline to correct me. Perhaps that was the trouble with my life. I needed someone to father me and a strong hand to guide me.

I'll never forget the first time I met my father and was old enough to understand who he was. I was just about ten and still living in Rockland Street. He arrived around tea-time one evening to pay Sarah the maintainance money she was due. It was coming up towards Christmas time and, as well as giving Sarah her regular money, he gave her a few pounds extra so that she could buy me a Christmas present.

He brought a food hamper too. It was nicely decorated on the outside with Christmas paper and inside it was well stocked with the best of good food. On top of the lot there was a fresh sprig of holly.

My father never stayed very long on those visits, just a few minutes, and he never sat down. He just stood in the doorway, his bulky frame silhouetted against the light ... and he always excused himself by stating how busy he was. Well ... he was a self-made millionaire, a shrewd business-man; and quite prepared to work long hours in the pursuit of financial success.

When he saw me that day he immediately turned to Sarah and asked, "Well, how is he?" "Ask him yourself," she said. "There he is!"

I think he spoke about two sentences to me and wished me a merry Christmas. His big deep voice frightened me and, as a child, I was always terrified of him. It seemed as if there was a wall between us so that I could never get close to him. I wonder if he ever felt that way?

Didn't he ever long to lift me up into his big arms and cuddle me as any father would a son? Didn't he ever wish he could take me fishing; or for a drive in his car? Didn't he ever wish he could make me a part of his immediate family? I wonder?

What sort of man would treat his own flesh and blood like this? After all, he has two other sons; both shareholders in his business; both well provided for and both enjoying the profits of his success. Why not me?

It's a strange thing! Even though I have met both the sons and have talked to them on the telephone, they don't know who I am. They don't know that we all have the same earthly father. I say it's a strange thing ... but sometimes, looking back, I remember how envious I was of all their material wealth and the lifestyle they enjoyed. Even now sometimes I feel the hurt because my father won't let me be a part of his family.

Looking back over the years and considering all the situations I have been in I recall the many times when I could really have used someone who cared about me.

I remember the time I was homeless and left Ulster in search of a new life in England. I sold everything I had for two hundred pounds but even before I set my foot on the boat half of the money had been drunk. My plan was to go to London. Maybe there I could find work ... and a home ... and happiness. But I only got as far as Liverpool and the whole trip lasted for little more than a week-end. I couldn't settle in England. Belfast was my home and I couldn't leave it.

It was around midnight when I stepped off the boat from Liverpool. I had nothing but the clothes I stood up in, about one pound fifty in cash ... and a mountain of worries. I was filled with anxiety, insecurity and uncertainty about my future. Where would a homeless and helpless lad go to find shelter? I could think of only one place ... the Salvation Army hostel, in Victoria Street, near the docks.

There were no vacancies on that night, however. The porter was friendly enough. He apologised for not being able to help me and then directed me to a men's hostel in the centre of town.

It's a long walk from Victoria Street to the city centre and at that time of the morning Belfast is always a cold place. But when you're ill-clad and hungry the cold night air bites in even deeper.

When I got to the hostel, the man on night duty wasn't going to let me in. Finally, when I was able to persuade him that I only wanted a bed for one night and wasn't going to give him any trouble, he opened the door. But it took ten minutes of talking through an intercom and then a while longer pleading through a chink in the partly opened door, held on a security chain, before he eventually gave in.

Over the next few months I went in and out of that shelter almost every day. It just so happened that it was directly opposite my father's business.

You can imagine the heartbreak I felt as, many a time, I stood at the window of that shelter, without so much as the price of a cup of tea in my pocket and watched my Father, a millionaire, driving in and out in his Rolls Royce.

I was so hungry in those days that I even ate chocolate from off the ground. I had been in almost every men's hostel in Belfast, unable to settle anywhere and always on the move. So perhaps you can understand why I felt so bitter then against my father. He had everything money could buy .. I was homeless. He had a family around him .. I had no-one. I felt so unwanted and so lonely. "If only he would love me!" I thought.

There had been another time, years before, when I had felt this same sense of loneliness. I was only about eight or nine years old at the time and Sarah was taken seriously ill. She had to go into hospital and I was sent to stay with friends.

Although they weren't blood relatives, I had grown up with these people and refered to them as aunt and uncle. They were very close to Sarah and had always felt sorry for me, being an orphan.

No one expected Sarah to be in hospital for very long but, as it turned out, including the time she was convalescing, she was there for eight weeks.

By the end of the eight weeks I felt that all was not well between me and the family I was staying with. As the weeks rolled on and there was no sign of Sarah getting out of hospital it seemed as if everyone began to act differently towards me.

Even at that tender age I could feel the tension rising. It was as if everybody was on a short fuse and the explosion would take place at any moment. For weeks on end I felt uneasy about my presence there. I was like an outsider who had overstayed his welcome and was living somewhere he didn't belong. Now I'm sure the family didn't want me to feel that way but I just did. I couldn't help it. Nothing in particular made me feel this way. It was just a lot of little things that, over a period of time, mounted up.

For example, every Friday when my uncle was giving out the pocket money he always gave my cousins more than he gave me. It wasn't a great deal more but it was enough to make me realize that I was different to his own sons.

My uncle used to play with his sons too, pretending to fight with them but, of course, never actually hurting them. It was great fun and the boys loved it. However, I only ever got to stand and watch. He never played with me. Naturally, I felt left out.

This increasing insecurity was added to by the behaviour of my cousins who used to laugh and giggle among themselves. I suppose it was all quite innocent but, at the time, I couldn't help thinking that they were laughing at me and it just added to my feelings of inferiority.

All these little things, coupled to the fact that I was really missing Sarah a lot, only added to my misery. Sometimes I would just sit and cry, not giving a reason, not even knowing why myself. I spent most of my childhood that way, unable to cope and becoming more and more insecure and lonely.

Loneliness has always been a big problem for me. Ever since my childhood I have allowed it to develop and, of course, it has resulted in fits of deep, black depression. The insecurity it has bred in me has become part of my every day make up and, added to my natural shyness, has often made life almost intolerable.

I have always been a very shy person and have found it difficult to cultivate friendships. Because of my upbringing and insecurity it's been hard to trust people in the way that you need to if friendships are to grow and blossom into anything permanent.

I've always had that fear of being hurt again and so have tended to keep a distance between myself and possible friends. I've always been very self conscious about my looks as well and felt that no-one would ever want me as a friend.

I suppose a lot of this was brought about by the fact that Sarah was a pensioner and very old fashioned in her ways. No matter how hard she tried she could never fully understand me. The generation gap between us was impossible to bridge. I was young and a bit of a tearaway and wanted to have fun. Sarah was old and settled and could never come to terms with the attitudes of modern youth.

All this resulted in me being brought up in a very sheltered way. The innocence of childhood continued well into my adolescence so that I was never properly taught what is commonly referred to as, "the facts of life."

The other kids in the street used to taunt me about this and make fun of my shyness and innocence. This led to frustration and confusion building up inside me. I would come running in to Sarah and explode in a tirade of abuse at her because she hadn't told me the things I needed to know.

Sitting alone in that prison cell, I realised how lost I was for friendship. If only there was someone in whom I could confide, someone who could understand me and whom I could trust. I was twenty-one years old now, no longer the little boy playing in the streets of Belfast, but I was still as lonely and insecure as I had ever been.

Yes .. not having a family was definitely having a bad effect on me. It was affecting my attitude to my mates in the prison too. They noticed that I was much more withdrawn and depressed.

I had sent visiting passes out, regularly, every week but just as regularly they met with no response. Week after week visiting time was, for me, disappointment time. No-one ever turned up.

The disappointment was magnified when the other prisoners excitedly told their stories of visiting time. I heard about girlfriends who were looking great, mothers who were complaining just for the sake of it and children who were sprouting up, like mushrooms, month by month.

It wasn't just the fact that my mates were getting visits and that I wasn't. There was more to it than that. I needed someone to identify with, someone to give me that sense of belonging and security.

This was probably the worst period of my life. Remanded in custody awaiting trial; no home to go out to; no family and no future. I longed for someone to give me hope!

CHAPTER SEVEN

WHERE SHALL THE SINNER FIND REST?

"COME UNTO ME ALLYE THAT LABOUR AND ARE HEAVY
LADEN AND I WILL GIVE YOU REST."
MATTHEW 11 v 28.

My depression was like a quick-sand into which I sunk deeper and deeper. It seemed never to go away. At one time it was so bad that I had even attempted suicide but I realised that taking my life was not the answer. If I had done so I would have come face to face with God ... and I wasn't ready for that. Oh, the gospel was no new thing to me. I knew the truth of it and at one stage had committed my life to Christ. But it was a shallow, empty profession and amounted to very little. At the time I was married to an attractive wee girl from Newcastle, Co. Down.

I met Michelle at a party which a few friends had thrown one night and, after going with her for a few weeks, invited her to come and live with me in our old house at Rockland Street.

After Sarah's death and my release from prison the first time, the Housing Executive had offered the house to me and since I didn't relish the idea of living on my own, I thought it would be great to have Michelle's company. I realise now that my reasons were purely selfish and that I had far more interest in my own comforts than in hers. Nevertheless, she came.

Right from the beginning, our relationship was a shaky one. Neither of us was very secure. Neither of us was capable of making a sensible, rational decision. As well as this we were both far too young. Nineteen is hardly a suitable age for getting married and taking upon yourself the possibility of having to raise a family, especially when you're as immature as we were.

But we were headstrong and determined. We allowed our hearts to rule our heads and four months later, in the registry office of Belfast City Hall, we were pronounced man and wife.

Not long after this we moved to Antrim, a decision which was forced upon us and undertaken in rather a hurry. The UDA had beaten me up one day in Rockland Street because I had been glue sniffing. As far as I'm concerned, I don't think that was the only reason, not even the main reason. There was a lot more to it.

At that time I had been involved in a personality clash with a fella who lived a couple of doors from us. There was also a lot of bitterness between myself and a number of old mates who used to call into the house regularly before Michelle came on the scene and put a stop to it. They felt that I had, as we say in Belfast, done the dirt on them and I suppose they felt a bit put out.

Anyway, they burst into the house one night, wrecked the living room, hurled abuse at Michelle and gave me a terrible hiding. In fact they left me in such a bad state that I was hardly recognizable.

Naturally, Michelle was terrified. She had never experienced the like before and her nerves were shattered by it. From that time onwards a knock at the door or the least wee noise would have her jumping out of her seat and wondering was the same thing going to happen again. And she would hardly leave the house unless I was with her.

We had already arranged a transfer with the Housing Executive, who seemed more than happy for us to move to Antrim. However, as it turned out, Antrim didn't do us any favours. There wasn't anything there for us and we seemed to spend most of the time fighting the bit out. It was an unemployment blackspot with more than half of the population on the dole queue. It seemed no wonder to us that it was referred to as the Housing Executive's dumping ground. We felt we had been dumped there!

After about three months in Antrim, Michelle and I were just about ready to kill each other. The pressure was too much for Michelle and every so often she would go running off back to her mother, leaving me to fend for myself. I, of course, had nowhere else to go and just had to make the best of it.

Eventually, shortly after discovering that she was pregnant, Michelle left for good. Then she did something that put the final nail in the coffin of our already shaky marriage. She either borrowed or was given money by her mother to have an abortion.

This was the final straw. It wasn't just that she had had an abortion. It was the fact that her mother had given her the financial wherewithal to do it ... without consulting me and on the condition that Michelle would have nothing more to do with me. Michelle's mother had long since branded me a hopeless case. And maybe at that time, as far as man was concerned, I was. But I felt that everyone had given up on me and felt so useless, hopeless and unwanted. No wonder the depression continued! Would my hopeless condition and pathetic situation never change? I could never have imagined how soon God was to step in and perform a modern miracle in my life.

●●●●●●●●●●

It was a Friday night in the middle of winter. I was very lonely and badly in need of a friend to talk to and so, to try and lift my mind, I went out for a walk. I hadn't gone far when I came across two young lads who were standing in the doorway of a house. They noticed me walking up and down aimlessly and came and introduced themselves. The young men were from the Church of God at Whitewell, in Belfast and they asked if they could come and talk to me about the Lord Jesus. I wasn't all that keen on hearing about religion but I was delighted at the prospect of having a bit of company for a while and so invited them down to the house for a cup of tea.

They stayed for about an hour that night, telling me of God's love for me and of how Christ died for me. And they said that if I would give my life to him I would not only be saved from Hell and damnation but would also have a true friend for life. You can imagine how the sound of those words appealed to me in my lonely and desperate condition.

Before they left, they showed me again the way of salvation, led me to Christ and knelt with me in the sinner's prayer. Then, just before they said good night, the taller of the two prayed again, asking God's blessing on my home. Immediately a great peace descended upon me, the like of which I had never experienced before. All my anxiety had suddenly gone. I didn't feel lonely anymore.

●●●●●●●●●●

Being a Christian was great at the start. I had really fallen in love with the Lord Jesus and, for the first time, began to enjoy going to church. I was reading the Bible with a new interest and continually learning new things about the

Christian life. As well as all this I was meeting lots of new friends. People I felt I could trust. People who cared about me. Everything was going well for me and for the first time in my life I felt content.

However, this happy situation was not to last for very long. I had always been a rather weak person. In fact, I would have described myself as being rather a mama's boy. In a word, gutless. Very soon I allowed temptation to get the better of me and instead of standing up for Jesus, as a good soldier, I took the easy path ... back to drink, drugs and glue sniffing. That was certainly a very foolish mistake. If I had maintained my walk with God I would never have found myself back in prison again.

••••••••••

Now here was I, a loyalist prisoner, in jail for fighting for my country, or so I imagined, and once again, alone. I hadn't been at all happy going my own way but, sadly, didn't have the courage to face up to the fact. Now that I was back in prison and amongst all these godless men how could I tell them that I was a backslider. My pride just wouldn't let me do it. As I sat there in 'A' wing, searching for an answer to my problems, all these thoughts bombarded my tortured mind.

During the three and a half months I had been on remand, the prison had seen many changes and it's whole mood had altered. The prisoners were no longer as militant towards the officers and all the protests and campaigns had ceased. Most of the guys who had been there when I came in had now gone but there was a constant stream of new faces.

A lot of men had gone for trial and had either been acquitted or sentenced. The ones who remained and were still awaiting trial were so caught up in what might happen to them that they had no time for anything, or anybody, else.

They were all so jittery! It was just like living in a big pressure cooker which didn't have a safety valve. I would be very glad to get out of it.

Easter would soon be upon us. . The courts were going flat out to clear the backlog of cases and that's why so many men were going for trial.

I hated Easter. There was even less to do than usual and for me it was an absolute bore. This was the case whether in jail or out of it. It was different this year, however. I was down deep in the valley of depression and just couldn't care less what happened. Surely things couldn't get any worse. Life could only get better.

I had asked one of the prison officers for a Bible and after about a week he arrived with it. It was in rather poor shape, covered in dust, dog eared at the corners and defaced with all manner of scribblings. But I welcomed it nevertheless. Its condition was immaterial just as long as it was readable.

I was eager to read the Bible again and hoped that it might bring me some lasting peace. Deep down within me, however, I knew that the only lasting answer was for me to yield my heart entirely to the Lord and to trust completely in him. But I still kept fighting that decision, trying by every other human means to find the peace that so eluded me.

It would be a good idea, I thought, to read the Bible from cover to cover. However, I had the wrong motive for thinking like this. I was still full of that old sin of pride and wanted to be able to boast that I had read the Bible right through. It was as if I was trying to notch up another credit to my account.

I started at the beginning, Genesis chapter one, verse one, and within a few weeks had got as far as the second book of Samuel.

But the reading of it didn't bring the peace I expected. In fact it made matters a whole lot worse because, as I read, its message convicted me. It made me more and more conscious of God - of his righteousness; his purity; his justice - and all that contrasted, so dramatically, with my impurity, my waywardness and my sin. I saw, more and more clearly, my need of salvation.

Coupled to this was the fact that I wasn't a very good reader. I had hated school and after my fourteenth birthday had very rarely been there. With an education such as mine you can imagine the problem I had struggling my way through those first few books of the Old Testament. The genealogies, in particular, gave me a lot of trouble. Some of the people there had names that sounded to me more like Welsh railway stations . It's a good job I wasn't a school teacher back in Bible times. By the time we had called the roll the children would have been looking for their lunch break!

My Bible reading was disturbed by the voice of a prison officer.

"Combined services, young Lawther," he said, shouting in through a slit in the partly opened the door.

He sort of took me by surprise for I had become so engrossed in my reading that I hadn't noticed the time going in. Once I had come to my senses and gathered my thoughts, I shouted back that I would be going to the service.

In fact I was really looking forward to it and to meeting a few old friends there. One man in particular I knew would be there. He was James McIlroy, the director of Prison Fellowship, Northern Ireland. I had known him for the past two or three years and had first been put in touch with him by the probation service when I lived in Antrim. He had helped me a great deal at the time Michelle had walked out.

I remembered how he used to call for me on his way from Randalstown, giving me a lift to Belfast and then bringing me back home again in the evening. I hadn't seen him in a long time but when I heard that he was coming to the prison church I was anxious to have a chat with him again.

By the time I made my way along to the service the hall, quite a large one, was packed. There were about a hundred and fifty men squeezed into the old wooden pews with prison officers positioned strategically around the walls.

At first the place sounded more like a cattle market with the babble of men's voices echoing off the hard plaster walls. There were men shouting to each other from each side of the hall and attempting to have conversations with their mates from other wings, whom they hadn't seen in a long time.

I had barely sat down, however, when the minister, the Rev. Jackson Buick, also the prison's Presbyterian chaplain, beckoned for everyone to be quiet. It took a few moments but, eventually, there was silence.

"Good afternoon men!" His voice was warm and inviting. "Welcome to our Easter services. We will be here again tomorrow and also on Friday which is, of course, Good Friday. We are here to try and show you the true meaning of Easter."

"About two thousand years ago the Lord Jesus left Heaven's glory and came down to this sin cursed world to die on a cross for the whosoever would believe. That's the good news we have come to tell you."

He then went on to introduce James McIlroy of the Prison Fellowship who, he told us, would soon be singing for us. Then he introduced a young man from the country, Noel Agnew, who would be doing the preaching.

Just at that point, Noel passed a funny comment about the way he was dressed and opened his jacket to reveal the old belt that held his trousers up. The lads enjoyed the joke. It gave them a laugh and helped them to relax.

They enjoyed his preaching too. He kept it down to earth and very simple and he threw in plenty of witty remarks as well. His theme that day was of the reality of death.

"It's one of the surest facts we ever have to face, and yet it's one of the most difficult to accept," he told us.

Noel peppered his sermon with a few anecdotes from an undertaker friend of his.. What a fund of stories that man had collected over the years. Most of his life was spent handling corpses - washing them, shaving them, dressing them, even putting make-up on some of them. All this, just to make a lifeless corpse look more presentable.

And then he remarked on some of the strange, even comical remarks you hear at wakes.

"Doesn't he look lovely, they say, referring to the corpse. But it's dead! It's lifeless! And if it's left long enough, it will stink!"

He made us all laugh again when he referred to the way some people look at the deceased in the coffin and say, "Doesn't he look awful like himself?" Well who else would he look like?

But then he brought us all back to reality very quickly with a verse from scripture. "It is appointed unto men once to die, but after this the judgment."

He put it very straight to us then. "You've only got one life to live. There are no second chances. This isn't a rehearsal. It's how you live this life now that will determine where you will spend the next. If you live it to please self and to satisfy your own desires it will be a complete waste, and you'll end up in a lost eternity. Live it to please God, live it to serve Christ, and it will bring you eternal happiness!"

I left the church service that day knowing exactly what I had to do. God had spoken to me once again and the message was unmistakable. I had to surrender my life and my will to Christ before it was too late.

I had been wrestling with this tug on my heart for weeks now but I was still too proud. I was frightened that my mates would laugh at me so, again, I put off that most important decision. The poet's words were all too true in my case. "Procrastination is the thief of time!"

It wasn't until some three weeks later that, still very proud, I did eventually commit my whole life to Jesus Christ. But it was not before an almighty struggle had taken place in that prison cell - and in my heart - between the powers of darkness and the powers of light.

It was one night after we had been locked up. I was feeling even more depressed than usual and just lay on my bed staring at the ceiling and wrestling with my thoughts. For hours I turned over and over again the various situations I had found myself in since the time I had backslidden from the Lord.

The conclusion I came to was that the only time I had been really happy was during those five or six months that I had lived as a Christian. At that time I was living in Antrim, attending the Whitewell church, mixing with other warm hearted believers and going on with the Lord. Those had been blessed days. They had been profitable days. But now they were gone and so too was the joy that had accompanied them.

As I lay in that prison cell, gazing at the ceiling and lamenting my sorry state, I started to pray. I told the Lord how sinful and foolish I had been to wander away from his straight paths. I told him how sorry I was. I even promised him - and I don't recommend this kind of bargaining with God - that if he got me out of this mess I was in, I would serve him for the rest of my life.

As I say, I don't recommend bargaining with God, for at least two reasons. First, God is not a man that he should be persuaded or cajoled by any promise we would make to him. Second, we should be very careful, and very serious about striking bargains with God. He just might hold us to the bargain - and then we could find ourselves really over a barrel.

God doesn't run his kingdom the way men run their businesses. If you make a bargain with God he may well give you exactly what you asked for - but nothing more. If, however, you serve him gladly and freely - and with no strings attached - he will give you abundantly and freely all that you need.

I know the Bible gives examples of men like Jacob who struck tough bargains with God. But they were made in the most extreme circumstances and only, I believe, after very serious thought. The Bible also warns us that, it is better not to vow, than to vow and not pay. So be careful. Don't follow my example just because it seemed to work for me.

Anyway, I sat up in my cell and quite simply asked the Lord back into my life again. I could hardly take in what followed. A great peace came flooding into my heart. So great that it almost took my breath away. An experience like that is impossible to put into words. What I will say is that in all my years of drinking, drug taking, parties and girls, none of those things ever gave me such a sense of satisfaction as I had in the prison cell that night.

It's true what the hymn says. "Where Jesus is, 'tis heaven there." That night a wee taste of heaven came down into my prison cell. My circumstances hadn't changed but I certainly had. From that moment my whole life began to improve and it wasn't very long till I was out of jail on bail.

CHAPTER EIGHT

GUILTY AS CHARGED

"ALL THESE EVIL THINGS COME FROM WITHIN AND
DEFILE THE MAN."
MARK 7 v 23

After being released on bail, I went to live in East Belfast.
The first thing I had to do was to report to the local R.U.C.
station so they could check that my bail release papers were
in order. When I was there, the police made it very clear to
me that, while I was on bail, my movements would be
somewhat restricted.

For example, I had to report to the police station every
Thursday evening at seven o'clock and sign the bail book.
I suppose this was to ensure that I hadn't skipped bail and
fled the country.

For the first few days after my release, I faithfully read
my Bible and prayed. However, since I didn't have any
other Christians to fellowship with, my enthusiasm soon
waned and I drifted back into my old ways. I wasn't like
your average new convert in a good local church with lots
of other young Christians as companions and older, mature
ones as guides. I didn't have an affiliation to any local
church. I didn't know any other Christians - at least none
living near me - and so I didn't attend church regularly.

That was a real problem. Since I didn't know anybody and since I was in such trouble with the law it made it difficult for me to walk in and attach myself to a good local church.

I'm not making excuses here nor am I trying to apportion blame to anyone else. These are just the facts of my case. I mention them only to stress to other young believers the importance of finding a place where you can enjoy the fellowship of other like minded people. I mention it too, that older Christians may realise that young, new born babes in the faith need to be nurtured and encouraged.

A famous Ulster evangelist, W.P. Nicholson, used to say, "You don't put young chicks under a dead hen!" By that he meant that those who are young and weak in the faith need the instruction and care of faithful Bible teachers and pastors. That's the only way they can be kept from being led astray by falsehood and the only way they can grow to spiritual maturity.

But I wasn't sitting under any kind of hen at all. I was alone. And being alone I didn't really stand a chance. My big problem was that having been saved in the prison I was cut off from any clear Bible teaching. I had no awareness of what the life of a believer should be like. I knew nothing about Christian discipline. I didn't even have any clear pattern of Bible reading. What chance did I have of succeeding as a Christian?

Now when you bear in mind all that I've said, it'll come as no surprise to learn that it wasn't long before the temptations of the world overcame me - and I was powerless to resist them.

I believe now that my powerlessness was a direct result of my lack of prayer. I wasn't living close to the Lord and so the drift into the ways of the world was inevitable. I started drinking again and found myself easily lured into ungodly conversation. Sadly, this trend continued for a few months until the time of my trial drew near.

Just a few days before the trial I went back up to Ballysillan to renew acquaintance with a few old friends. One of these was a man called Roy Montgomery. Our reunion took me completely by surprise.

The first thing Roy did, after we had shaken hands and said hello, was to announce that he had become a Christian. I was astounded by this news. Roy - a Christian!

Roy and I had been good friends for years. He and I had both belonged to the same political party. We had worked side by side in the party's advice centre. We lived in the same housing estate and many a time had spent hours at his place discussing party politics till the wee small hours. And we were old drinking mates too!

But now he was a completely changed man. No longer did his ambitions lie in the pursuit of party politics but in the extending of Christ's kingdom and in the glorifying of his name. It was amazing! It was incredible! But it was to be a great blessing to me.

Roy listened sympathetically while I poured out my frustrations and fears - especially the fear of having to go back into prison again, and he faithfully promised that, when the time came for me to appear on trial, he would be there with me.

I told him how lonely I had been while in prison, on remand, without anyone to visit me, and again he assured me that if I was given a prison sentence this time he would visit me regularly.

After chatting for a while Roy, invited me down to his flat for a bite to eat, and there he related the story of his conversion. His life-style hadn't been bringing him the happiness he expected. In fact, over the years he had sunk into deep depression - a depression that manifested itself in what felt like a great lump in his chest - and which kept him from sleeping.

Like the woman in the Bible with the issue of blood, he had tried everywhere for a cure but to no avail. As a last resort he contacted the pastor of the local Elim church, Jackie McKee, who led him into the personal experience of Jesus Christ as saviour. Since then the Lord had done great things for him. He was a new man.

While listening to Roy I couldn't help thinking of my own situation. I, too, had made a commitment to the Lord but all I ever seemed to do was to let him down. I shared this with Roy and he did a lot to help and encourage me.

He explained that, even though I had failed the Lord, it didn't mean the Lord had stopped loving me. Christ was still my saviour, I was still his child and it was never too late to start living for him.

Roy offered to pray for me and said he would get the church members to pray for me too. I asked him again if he would go with me to the court on the day of the trial and he assured me he would. We said good night on much better terms than ever before and I felt that here was a true friend I could trust.

●●●●●●●●●●

On the morning of my trial I was very nervous. I hadn't slept a wink the night before and, consequently, wasn't able to think straight. For days my mind had been occupied with court rooms, lawyers, judges and the possible sentence I might have to serve.

By now it was nine o'clock and I was absolutely exhausted. The cold shower and shave hadn't really done much for my appearance, which spoke more of sleepless nights and worry. During the past six months on bail my weight had dropped dramatically so that the old denims, which at one time would hardly meet around my middle, needed a belt to hold them up.

I set off for the court dressed in denim jacket and jeans, sweatshirt and trainers, with my tobacco tin and lighter in the top pocket. As I pulled the front door behind me I was certain it would be a long time before I would be back again.

The walk across town to the Crumlin Road court-house was like a convicted prisoner's last walk along death row. My heart weighed heavy, my feet dragged and I moved along, step by trembling step, in a complete daze. Now and then I was aware of others passing by and greeted them with a, "Good morning", or a brief comment about the weather. But in fact I had no interest in anything that was happening about me. I could think only of my impending doom.

I arrived at the court-house far too early - ten to ten - the court didn't sit till a quarter to eleven. What would I do? Would I go for a walk to pass the time or would I go and wait inside. As I stood there grappling with this otherwise simple decision my friend Roy Montgomery arrived.

"Good morning mate," he said as soon as we met. "How are you doing?" I was very nervous and told him so. "Och, you'll be all right son," he assured me.

"I don't know about that Roy. This could go either way and if I get a bad result I could end up with double figures this time."

"We've all been praying for you," Roy said. "Our pastor mentioned it again last night at the evening meeting. He said if you do happen to get time he'll be up to see you on a pastoral visit. That should give you some hope."

I said I'd be grateful for that but still I was worried. The thought of going back into Crumlin jail for a longer spell didn't appeal to me at all.

Since Roy had got saved he had been going to the Elim church in Ballysillan. He loved it and was always telling me about it. I felt as though I knew the people there, although I'd never met any of them except Roy, but his enthusiasm was infectious. "If ever I get out of prison that's where I'll be going," I thought.

Up to this point I'd never met the barrister who would be defending me, although the solicitor had assured me that he had been fully briefed about my case and had been kept up to date with all its developments. Still, I hadn't made personal contact with the barrister and that also worried me a bit.

Fifteen minutes before the court went into session he came and introduced himself to me. He sounded very positive.

"You've got a good judge today, Judge Petry. I believe if you go into the court and throw your hands up - plead guilty - throw yourself at the mercy of the court you'll get no more than four years.

"What if I don't?" I replied. "Then you'll get another judge who might not be as lenient and you could end up with more than eight years - possibly ten."

I agreed to plead guilty to the charges and to hope and pray that everything would turn out all right. The barrister complimented me on being very wise and then went on to ask me some questions about my background and family circumstances. Finally he asked if there was anything else he ought to know before we went into court. I just shook my head, indicating that there wasn't.

"I'll see you in court then," he said and left.

The court-room was very small. There was only enough room in the public gallery for three or four people so everyone was a bit cramped. That is everyone except me. I had a seat all to myself - in the dock - with a prison officer at either end blocking the way in case I tried to escape.

I sat there for a few minutes - daydreaming - but very quickly snapped out of it when the clerk of the court suddenly boomed out, "All stand," and the judge entered.

It was a very sobering moment. What would happen to me?

The judge solemnly took his seat and the trial began. It was then that I really became nervous. So nervous, in fact, that I was overtaken by a compulsion to giggle at almost every word spoken. Even as the charges - and they were very serious - were read out I couldn't breathe properly for fear of bursting out in a fit of giggling. I know it sounds funny now but it was anything but funny at the time. It was sheer nervousness.

I did have the presence of mind to pray about the situation and asked the Lord to help me. Miraculously, and thankfully, in a short time I calmed down again and was able to pay attention to what was happening.

In fact, I have never been so calm in a court since then, even though I've been before many other judges. It was just amazing and I attribute it all to the Lord who made his presence known to me that day. He completely took away all my fears and renewed my confidence.

The trial itself took only forty-five minutes and most of that time was spent in listening to the evidence of the police.

They explained that, when they raided a house in the Oldpark Road area of Belfast, they had been acting on information received. The house had been occupied by me at the time and the detective went on to describe how that, after a thorough search of the premises, they had uncovered a firearm - a .22 Colt pistol which was in working order and ready to be fired.

They had also uncovered forty-five rounds of ammunition, some of which fitted the pistol. The ammunition was in a lunch box which had been greased to keep out damp. They then went on to report how I had been arrested the following morning, at five-thirty, in a men's hostel near the city centre.

Several policemen gave evidence, and in turn, were cross examined by my barrister. I must say he did his job marvellously, sifting into all the evidence and leaving no stone unturned. He was probably the best barrister I've ever had to represent me.

The detective who gave most of this evidence was, in fact, in charge of the men who had interrogated me in Castlereagh holding centre. He had a certain degree of sympathy for me because I didn't have a family. He was also convinced that I wasn't either a ring leader or a so called God-father.

He was more of the opinion that I was simply a gofor, someone who took orders and did whatever he was asked without question - and perhaps without even thinking. He thought my motivation was more fear than anything else.

Because of all this, when he had finished giving his evidence, he spoke a few words in my favour saying that I was probably just a victim of circumstances. He felt that I had learned my lesson and that if given the opportunity I wouldn't have anything more to do with para-militaries. He even went as far as to say that if I was set free on this occasion I wouldn't re-offend.

The judge, meanwhile, was making up his own mind. As I sat there in the dock, just listening and observing, I could see him every so often lifting his eyes from off his notes and looking over at me. I suppose he was watching the expression on my face as various things were said, particularly when the detective spoke in my favour. I made sure not to look too confident but to adopt more an air of repentance, in the hope that the court would be merciful.

Finally all was said and done. Every scrap of evidence had been presented. Everything, both in my favour and against, had been said. It was time for the judge to announce his decision. What would the verdict be?

I was ordered to stand and the prison officers on either side of me moved in closer. Did they think I was about to make a run for it? Or were they making sure I wouldn't get a chance to throw anything at the judge? Others had done that in the past. Of course I had neither in mind. I would take my medicine, whatever it was, and do my time if I had to.

The judge began, as is the custom, with his summing up speech. He agreed that I did have a lot going for me and that I wasn't fully to blame for the events that had taken place. He realised that there were more sinister elements involved in this case who, unfortunately, were not before the court today to answer for their misdeeds. I had certainly been manipulated and taken advantage of by these people but that didn't absolve me from blame. I had broken the law and, therefore, must be punished for it.

By this time I thought it wasn't looking too good for me. I saw a long stretch in prison looming up. It was even more serious than I had thought. But then the judge announced the sentence. What a shock!

"On the charge of possession of a firearm - eighteen months imprisonment. And on the other two charges of possession of ammunition with intent to endanger life - eighteen months imprisonment. Both charges to run concurrently."

Well ... I could hardly believe my ears - and I could hardly contain my relief. Eighteen months! It could easily have been eighteen years and the court would have been well justified in handing out such a sentence.

Possession of firearms or ammunition with intent to endanger life has on some previous occasions carried a life sentence. Yet here I was with a sentence of only eighteen months. It was nothing short of a miracle. Surely God had heard and answered prayer. Surely he had shown mercy and dealt graciously with me. I, Graham Lawther, did not get what I deserved. Did I not have a lot to be thankful for?

As soon as the sentence had been announced the clerk gave the order for all to stand while the judge left and the court was cleared. That took about ten minutes and I had to wait there until the court-room was empty before they could bring me out.

Most court-rooms have a staircase or an adjoining door that leads conveniently and privately to a tunnel that runs between Crumlin court-house, on the one side of the road and the prison on the other. However, this one didn't so I had to wait. But that was a good thing really because it meant that I would have to exit right past the public gallery where Roy, who had been there for the whole hearing, was waiting.

I didn't really have to say anything to him - my face said it all. Of course I was absolutely delighted with the sentence and just couldn't contain my joy. I was grinning like a Cheshire cat!

"Well you did all right chum," said Roy. "Brilliant!" I replied, then muttered something like, "Praise the Lord. He has been so good to me."

I asked Roy if he would come and see me in prison as soon as possible. He said he would come in a day or two, as soon as I had settled in. "Well thank everyone for praying for me and ask them to keep it up."

No sooner had Roy agreed to do that than the prison officer came and led me away. On the way over to the prison I couldn't keep quiet and chatted away to the officer telling him how fortunate I had been in getting so short a sentence. He wasn't at liberty to say a whole lot but he agreed that I had been let off rather lightly.

Just before he locked me away he asked if I'd like some lunch. Well the events of the last hour or two had given me a great appetite so I replied, "Aye."

"Right then, I'll see what I can do for you," and he walked away leaving me alone in the cell.

During those quiet moments alone my thoughts were a combination of relief that the trial was over and the result was so good; of joy that my term in prison would be so short; and of fear, for remember I had promised God that if he extricated me from the mess I was in I would serve him faithfully.

But I had never lived out and out for God in the atmosphere of prison before. How would I face up to this challenge? What temptations would be set before me? And where would the strength come from to stand apart from the crowd? These were questions that would only be answered in time.

CHAPTER NINE

A CHRISTIAN WITHOUT POWER!

"WHEREFORE BY THEIR FRUITS YE SHALL KNOW THEM."
MATTHEW 7 v 20.

Up until now, my only experience of prison had been either while on remand or in the young offender's centre. 'D' wing was quite different. Since I had never been sentenced before, it was all new to me and my first impressions were none too good. In fact it was rather disgusting.

The differences between being on remand and being sentenced were soon to become obvious. But immediately I was confronted with the fact that there was much less privacy for a man who has been sentenced. The privileges were not the same either.

I was put into a cell with two other men. The cell had originally been meant to hold one man and it had neither the space nor the facilities for three. There was no toilet, of course, just three chamber pots, so you can imagine how the place stank. The smell of urine, excreta and unwashed feet hung in the air continually.

The other two men weren't Christians and, men being men, they had covered the notice board with pin-up pictures of girls, naked to the waist. There were a few obscenities scribbled on the walls too. To make matters worse, the cell itself was the last one on a long landing so it seemed as if you were exiled from everyone else. Also, it's position obscured any possible view.

There was a very good reason for this which I found out later. The other two men with whom I shared the cell were both paramilitary commanders and had a very tough reputation in the prison. They were both currently serving short sentences for comparatively minor offences but much more serious charges were pending.

One of them was in the UDA and was awaiting trial for the biggest arms robbery ever to take place in Ulster. He and three other men had dressed up as members of the Ulster Defence Regiment. (The U.D.R. is a regiment of the British Army whose sole responsibility is security in the province.) The three of them drove a van into a U.D.R. base and stole hundreds of rifles, machine guns, ammunition and hand grenades. However, after a lengthy car chase, they were apprehended near their destination in Belfast.

The other man was a member of the UVF awaiting trial on charges of armed robbery at a post office somewhere in the country.

At the beginning, these two men were very hard to get along with. They probably resented me being there, as it were, invading their privacy. Before my arrival they could talk freely but now, since I had come along, they had to watch what they said. They may have been saying things that my ears shouldn't hear.

It seemed as if they were trying to suss me out - to see what sort of stuff I was made of. I remember one particular conversation we had just after I had been in prison a short time. They had asked me what I was in for, and when I told them, they wanted to know what paramilitary team I belonged to. After quizzing me for a while they were able to tell me why we were all together in this particular cell.

"This is a top security cell and we're all in here to keep us out of the way. They don't want any trouble and they don't want us to get the chance to start a protest or anything of that nature. This is the only cell on this wing where everyone is a loyalist paramilitary and in for political offences."

My Christian witness in the prison was non-existent. After a full week on 'D' wing I hadn't told anyone that I was a christian, nor had I asked for a Bible. In Proverbs, Solomon wrote, "The fear of man bringeth a snare," and that was very true in my case. I just couldn't bear to face the humiliation that I would be subjected to if I told these hardened, godless men that I was a simple believer in the Lord Jesus.

Looking back, I realise what a hypocrite I was. To think that the Son of God came to this earth and died a lonely, shameful death on the Cross for me, to save me from my sins - and I didn't have enough courage to ask for a Bible. What pride filled my heart! How unworthy I was!

Quite a few weeks of my sentence had been served before I made any open confession of Christ and, even then, it came about quite unexpectedly. You could say it was more or less wormed out of me.

I had been put to work in the prison kitchen along with three other men. One of these was a chap called Benny Edwards. He was one of the so called Shankill butchers and was doing life for three murders. Later, he became a good friend of mine.

Anyway, the four of us were working together this day at the baking table and, during a tea break, were talking together about this and that - but nothing in particular. However, out of the blue, one of them said to me, "Are you a Christian?"

I was completely flabbergasted and didn't reply immediately. As I considered how I would answer, he continued.

"You never curse or nothin'!"

I still searched for words. I know I should have replied right away, without hesitation and it's to my shame that I didn't. But it just lets you see how low I had sunk spiritually. I was ashamed to stand up boldly and be counted for the Lord.

At the time, I felt I had made some sort of deal with the Lord. I wasn't strong enough to confess him openly before men but I felt I was doing my best. I wasn't swearing. I wasn't telling dirty jokes. It was as if I was doing Jesus some sort of favour. But now I realised it wasn't enough. These men had noticed the difference in my conduct, such as it was and now they were asking me, just where I stood.

Eventually, after what seemed a lot of stuttering and stammering, I got out that indeed I was a Christian. What a relief! As soon as I got the words out, a tremendous sense of relief came over me and a great peace flooded my heart. The response from the other men wasn't what I expected either.

They didn't laugh. They didn't make fun of me or refer to me as a holy Joe. In fact they were very understanding, even sympathetic.

"We knew you were," one of them said. "There have been hundreds of Christians in here over the years. You get to know the signs after a while."

It wasn't long before everybody in 'D' wing knew that I was a Christian. My mates were shocked, especially those who had been on remand with me in 'A' wing. Some of them even thought I was up to something. But after a while, when they saw the consistency of my conduct, they realised I was serious.

But at the same time, I was far from being the person I should have been. I was still selfish and proud. There was a spiritual laziness about me and discipline and spiritual growth were virtually non-existent.

Of course the reason for this was very simple. I wasn't getting any proper, sound Bible teaching. My view of Christ and his salvation was all wrong. I had received him as my saviour all right and was in no doubt about the fact that my sins were forgiven. I had the hope of heaven and a certain measure of God's peace within my heart. But I still wasn't prepared to give Jesus Christ full control of my life - to make him Lord.

There's an old saying that a lot of preachers have quoted many times. "If Christ is not Lord of all - he is not Lord at all." I think that that was my basic problem back in those days. Sometimes I think I resembled those of whom Paul speaks in 2 Timothy Ch. 3 v 5. "Having a form of Godliness but denying the power thereof." I was a professing christian all right but I behaved more like the ungodly than a child of God.

It wasn't that living as a Christian in 'D' wing was all that difficult. There were no particular hardships that I could list. No real opposition - and certainly no persecution.

The other prisoners soon got used to the fact that I was a Christian and their joking and laughter petered out. Only now and again, if they came across me reading my Bible, would they come out with a smart remark or a crude comment about some of the Bible characters. That used to get to me. It made me angry and it hurt. But I was very rarely ever man enough to do anything about it.

Every so often a few of them would call me by some nickname. Never anything very original. "Holy Joe," or "Bible thumper." But these never annoyed me. They were only to be expected. After all didn't Jesus say, "If they call the master of the house Beelzebub, what shall they not call his servants?"

What I found a bit more difficult was the way that some of the prisoners tried to put me on the spot by blaming God for the situations they found themselves in.

One particular prisoner, referred to as 'Crazy Joe,' and serving life on a charge of manslaughter, stopped me one day and said, "That's some God you've got, putting me in here to rot in this hole."

"It wasn't God who put you in here," I replied. "You're in here as a result of your sin."

"But who made me sin?" he retorted.

I did my best to explain how Adam, placed by God in the garden of Eden, had forfeited his right to paradise through his disobedience. Every generation since then has inherited Adam's sinful nature and has continued in Adam's disobedience and rebellion against God.

"So it's all Adam's fault then? Wait till I get my hands on him," he exclaimed. "I'll fix him for putting me in here!"

I've already explained that part of the reason for my immaturity as a Christian was the lack of good, sound Bible teaching. Because of the way the prison system works, it wasn't possible to pick and choose the meetings you could attend. You had to go to the ones that were made available to you and they weren't always the best.

The main prison service was on Sunday mornings. It was conducted on alternate weeks by the two prison chaplains, Rev. Jackson Buick, Presbyterian, and the Rev. Barry Dodds, Church of Ireland.

Most of the men who attended the Sunday morning service made no profession of faith, so the sermons didn't contain much of a doctrinal or spiritually educational content. They were more geared to showing men the way of salvation. This meant that I wasn't getting much teaching or direction in the christian walk and as a consequence, experienced very little spiritual growth.

The mid-week Bible study was much more beneficial, however, especially when led by the Rev. Buick. Over the course of the five months that I spent in 'D' wing, Mr. Buick's Bible study was to help me in so many ways and it was there that I got my first opportunity to share my testimony with others. As well as that Mr. Buick was to become a very close friend and a man for whom I still have the highest respect.

The giving of my testimony for the first time is a story in itself. On the day before it, I was so excited and had spent as much time as possible in prayer about it. I made a point of going around all my old friends and inviting them to the meeting. When I told them that I would be giving my testimony many of them didn't know what I was talking about. Others warned me to be very careful. They thought I'd be talking about some of the inner secrets of the UVF and perhaps spilling the beans on a few people.

However, I soon set the record straight and put them at their ease. Standing up to my full height and, I suppose, with a good deal of pride and self righteousness I explained that a testimony wasn't just a confession of one's wrongs. It was a public profession of Jesus Christ as saviour. That's what I was going to do.

All this was said in a rather boastful way as though to impress them with what I had learned since my conversion. In reality I had learned very little.

That lack of learning is well illustrated in what happened next. Something else had been troubling me for quite a while and now, I thought, was the time to put it right.

There had never been a communion service held in Crumlin jail and I thought that that was rather a shame. There were a good few believers in the prison but they had never been given the opportunity to meet together to break bread around the Lord's table.

The chaplains had a very sound explanation for this. Most of the men who were in prison weren't born again christians. It would be wrong to offer them the opportunity to partake of the symbols of Christ's death, the bread and the wine, and thus to have them run the risk of, in the words of the apostle Paul, "eating and drinking damnation to their souls." Far better, they thought, to exclude everybody than to have men doing that which was contrary to scripture.

But I had other ideas and intended to go through with my plan and to see it fulfilled on the same night as I gave my testimony.

First, I went along to the tuck shop and bought a bottle of blackcurrant cordial. You've already guessed what that was for. Then I managed to keep aside a couple of rounds of bread from the kitchen. Now don't be thinking that I stole them. I didn't! You see, now and again, those of us who worked in the kitchen were allowed to make ourselves a sandwich for supper. I just took my two rounds of bread and didn't put either butter or cheese on them. I wanted them specifically for the breaking of bread service. There was just one more problem. How would I tell the Rev. Buick?

I was quite worried about this for, as I have said, I had a great respect for Mr. Buick and didn't want to do anything that would offend him. I loved him very much in the Lord, valued his friendship a lot and would never normally have dreamt of doing anything to offend him. But this was different. I had a conviction about this and believed with all my heart that it was of God. So, come what may, I intended to go through with it.

When the time came for the meeting the welfare room was packed to capacity and they had to bring in extra seating to accommodate the overflow. In fact, the principal officer came in and informed Rev. Buick that the number of prisoners exceeded the limit set down by the prison authorities. However, Mr. Buick assured him that everything was well under control and the meeting was allowed to proceed.

The Rev. Buick then took me aside and asked if I was all set to give my testimony. I replied that I was, indeed that I had been looking forward to it for some days.

"I see you've brought some friends with you," he said, turning and referring to the extra men in the room.

"Yes," I replied. "I've been telling them that I'd be giving my testimony and have asked them to come along."

"Well, they're very welcome."

Just then he noticed the bread and the cordial. "I see you've brought your lunch with you too."

I was a bit nervous about answering him but managed to blurt out my plan.

"And before you say anything, Jackson, I believe this to be of the Lord. None of the lads in here who are believers ever get a chance to break bread together and we've been here nearly three and a half months now. So I took it upon myself to get the bread and the cordial so we could have it tonight."

I fully expected him to be angry with me and was half prepared for his rebuke. But he reacted in a different way altogether. He was surprised but didn't say a word for a few moments. Then he just calmly informed me that if the Lord had laid on my heart to do this, far be it from him to offer any discouragement.

"We will hear your testimony first though. Then if anyone wants to leave they can do so."

It took me about fifteen minutes to give my testimony. That was much less time than I had anticipated, although I suppose it was long enough. All the things I had planned to say about the UVF were forgotten - my mind went blank on those matters - and I spent the time simply telling the other men what the Lord had done for me. What little scripture I did know came readily to mind and through that I was able to speak of Christ and his power to save.

There was none of the old boastful self, which surprised me. It was just as if the Lord had given me a special touch for the occasion. Indeed, I'm sure he did. This was something I had never done in my life before, sat with a group of men and told them of their need of a saviour. I felt, at last, that I had really done something worth while for the kingdom of God.

In the Old Testament God used a dumb ass to deliver his message. Here, in the Crumlin Road prison in Belfast, he had used another kind of dumb ass for his purpose again. There was no doubt in my mind that the Lord had put the words into my mouth and that he had used them for his own glory. And I could see that the men were moved by what they heard.

After I had given my testimony we sang a hymn and then the Rev. Buick led us in the breaking of bread service. What a glorious time it was. Never before had I experienced such a sense of the presence of God. The prison bars and locks were able to keep us in but they couldn't keep the Spirit of God out. The Rev. Buick himself said he had never known a time when the blessing of God was so evident in a prison service.

•••••••••

Through my conversion I met many new friends, one of whom was Jackie McKee, the pastor of Ballysillan Elim church. Roy Montogmery had told him of me and he had come to see me in prison on a pastoral visit. Over a period of time he came to visit me quite regularly and through those visits our relationship grew and our friendship was bonded.

During one of the visits pastor McKee suggested that it might be a good idea if I could give my testimony in his church at a midweek service. I, of course, was delighted at the idea but didn't see much prospect of it ever happening, at least not until I had served my full prison term.

But then the news came of my release on parole, for forty-eight hours, from Monday to Wednesday. I would spend the time in Roy Montgomery's house and give my testimony on the Tuesday evening. The date was set; all the arrangements were made and the people told that I would be there to speak.

I remember it as though it was yesterday. The meeting was billed as a mid-week special with both Roy and myself giving testimony. They even booked a singer too. The small church was packed to capacity and the atmosphere in the place was, as they say, electric!

Roy gave his testimony first, taking about thirty minutes and then there were two beautiful solos from the singer. Then it was my turn.

It wasn't like giving my testimony in the prison. On that occasion I just sat in the middle of the group of men and talked to them. But in the church I had to stand in the pulpit before a crowd of about one hundred and eighty people. That gave me a great sense of importance and I'm afraid it rather spoiled the effect.

I spoke for a full forty-five minutes and to tell you the truth, most of it was waffle. I was very self centred, boastful and full of pride. I felt as if I hadn't given the glory to the Lord, although a lot of the people afterwards said that I had.

It was clear to me that I had a long, long way to go before God could ever use me effectively. There was still an awful lot of the old man in me and it wasn't long before I realized what it was to be rebuked for it. However, it was a good learning experience and one that I'll never forget. Next day I returned to the prison to serve out the remainder of my sentence.

CHAPTER TEN

CHRISTMAS PAROLE

"MY GOD SHALL SUPPLY ALL YOUR NEED ACCORDING TO HIS RICHES IN GLORY BY CHRIST JESUS"
PHILIPPIANS 4 v 19.

The queue seemed to be going nowhere. It was ages since the last man had been called. Time was dragging in - every minute seemed more like the passing of an hour. How I wished they would hurry up. It surely can't take that long to let somebody out of jail. What on earth could be keeping them?

This was Christmas parole and I was one of the fortunate ones - getting out of Crumlin prison for the holiday. There were about twenty of us waiting in different cells and I must have been near the bottom of the list.

The men were called three at a time and then taken down to reception for the necessary checks. Part of this was a search and it entailed stripping off so that each piece of clothing could be inspected individually.

Next came the reading of the riot-act by one of the prison officers. The riot-act, as we called it, consisted of a recital of all the do's and don'ts of being on parole. For us there were more don'ts than do's. Don't have too much strong drink! Don't get into bad company! And above all - don't be late back! Actually, it took about ten minutes for each man but, on days like this, there were usually a few officers laying down the law and so a little time was saved.

I was in a cell with four other blokes, all waiting to be called. There was great excitement in the atmosphere and everyone was bubbling over with joy at the prospect of a few days freedom. Of course, the conversation centred around what we'd all be doing once the prison gates closed behind us. Some had already decided what pub or club they'd be going to. Others mentioned the name of that lucky girl who'd have the pleasure of their company for the few days. And of course, as you'd expect in a cell full of men whose lives seemed to centre around drink and sex, there was plenty of dirty talk.

By the time the conversation came around to me I was already feeling pretty uncomfortable. I had no interest in hearing about the fine detail of the other men's prospective sex lives. In fact, I found it very embarrassing. But it was as if I was being lured into a conversation of which I wanted no part.

"What about you, Grahamer? What will you be up to?" asked one big fellow called Billy.

He and I worked in the kitchen together and he knew about my Christian profession. However, he had also known me before we came into prison and we were mutually friendly with a lot of the same people - fellas and girls. He began to make fun of me over one particular girl whom he said I had been out with. It so happened that I'd never been out with this girl so, in the absence of any foundation to the story, the jesting soon came to an end.

The conversation and the joking were finally brought to a halt when the prison officers came to our cell to take us down to reception.

The scene in reception was near enough to mayhem. Officers in short sleeved shirts marched to and fro, shep-

96

herding prisoners through the security checks as quickly as possible. The prisoners themselves were overcome with excitement and there was the constant babble of voices as men called to each other across the room.

The checks on me were straightforward enough. A quick look at my security photograph; an examination of my tattoos; and a couple of questions - like date of birth and address. Then there was the riot act which, for me, took about three minutes flat and must have been a record.

It was only a few minutes more till I heard the welcome voice of one of the officers calling out, "Open number one gate!"

I stepped out on to the busy Crumlin Road, a free man for a while and was met with a big hug from my good friend Roy Montgomery.

When we arrived at Roy's house I had hardly sat down till he asked if I'd like a fry. I can tell you he didn't have to ask twice. The food in the prison, as I've already indicated, was never fantastic but their fries were a particular disaster. To me a fry's no good unless it comes with a runny egg. But, in prison, the eggs were so hard I had the feeling that if you dropped one it would bounce back up at you.

Well I got my fry, complete with dipped soda, potato bread - and there was a runny egg too. It was delicious and just the thing to set a man up for the rest of the day. Dinner at the plushest hotel in the land wouldn't have tasted any better.

Roy's home was a little heaven to me for those few days. Apart from the cheery fire in the grate, which drove the bitter morning cold out of my bones, there was a real homely atmosphere in the house and Pat, Roy's wife, was a perfect hostess. I don't think that any couple could have made me feel more welcome during that short parole than Roy and Pat Montgomery. The way they opened up their home to me and the love and kindness they showed me are things I'll remember for the rest of my life and will be eternally grateful for.

"Are you in Roy?" came the voice from the front door which was lying ajar.

"Aye, come on in Freddie." Roy recognised the voice of Freddie McKeown, a friend of his who lived a short distance away.

Freddie was a Christian too, with a background similar to my own, except he had never been to jail. He also attended Ballysillan Elim church and had been there on the night I had given my testimony. He had been kind enough then to come and encourage me and to say how the Lord had spoken to him through my experience.

Long before this, we had been casual acquaintances and now and again had enjoyed the odd drink together. But we could never have been described as close friends. Little did I know that in due course he would become one of my closest friends and a real pillar of strength in times of trouble.

As soon as Freddie stepped into Roy's living room he had a hearty handshake and a cheery greeting for me.

"How're you doing Graham? I suppose you're glad to be out!"

"You'd better believe it, I've been really looking forward to it," I replied.

Just then Roy's wife, Pat, came in. She had been out shopping and as soon as she saw me she said, "Hi ya, bird! They let you out then!"

Roy interrupted. "They threw him out. They couldn't stick him. He had all their heads turned."

I was really enjoying the crack, as we say in Belfast. This was going to be a great few days.

Very soon Freddie had to go but, before he left, he reminded me of the young people's carol service the following night - Christmas eve - and invited me to come along. He said I could come up to the pastor's house afterwards for a cup of tea and a time of fellowship too. I said I'd try to be there.

"Aye do," said Freddie. "You'll enjoy it. You always get a good laugh at the pastor's house. See you later!" he announced, and disappeared out the door.

Pastor Jackie McKee was a young man in his mid thirties. I had been looking forward to meeting him and discussing my plans for the future. I was looking forward to the fellowship with other young Christians too. It would do me a lot of good, I thought. Sadly, I also looked upon it as an opportunity to do a bit of showing off.

Anyway, I arrived at pastor McKee's house about an hour early. I wanted to have plenty of time to chat to him without being disturbed. I soon discovered that the pastor was quite a character and very witty at times. But it was also obvious that he had a great love for the Saviour. And he was not just a dedicated Christian, he was a very knowledgeable one too. Two years at Bible college and a further ten in the ministry had seen to that.

He listened quietly and patiently as I related my experiences in prison. We discussed my cell mates; the problems of trying to live as a Christian in prison; the temptations and stumbling blocks that Satan placed before me; my career plans after I would be released and even where I would live.

Pastor McKee was sympathetic to my situation; encouraged me to develop a closer walk with the Lord; to entrust everything to him and assured me of the help and prayers of the church members after my release.

The hour slipped in very quickly and we were just enjoying a cup of coffee, provided by the pastor's wife, when the door bell rang. It was the young people back from the carol service.

They swept into the room like a breath of fresh air - all laughing and joking about the parts of the service that didn't go quite according to plan and ribbing each other as to who was and who wasn't in tune. There was a great sense of life about them and it was obvious they had enjoyed themselves.

What most impressed me about them was the fact that they were having so much fun and yet it was all so innocent and pure. They didn't need drink, or drugs, or discos, or illicit sex. They had the joy of the Lord in their hearts and it gave them complete satisfaction. You could tell that by the expression on their faces. Life to them was just great and they had no intention of swapping what they had for the transient pleasures of the world.

I met a lot of new friends that night, people whom I felt comfortable with and whom I still value greatly to this day.

Back in Roy's home that night I was a much happier man. The peace that the Bible speaks of in Philippians 4 v 7 filled my heart and truly for me it, "passed all understanding." Roy was in good form too. We spent a good while talking together about what the Lord had done for us and sharing our blessings. But, of course, I still took every opportunity to boast about myself.

At that time Pat, Roy's wife, was still unsaved but very interested in the things of God and, as it turned out, not far from the kingdom. She joined the conversation and we chatted together until almost midnight when Roy, who worked for a local taxi firm, had to leave to go on duty.

I was awakened next morning, Christmas day 1987, by the sound of footsteps on the stairs and the living room door opening. When I came down stairs Pat was in the kitchen making tea and she offered me a cup. As I sat there sipping it, my thoughts moved forward to the day ahead and what lay in store for me. I had mixed feelings about it.

On the one hand I was relieved to be out of prison for a while but on the other, Christmas had never appealed much to me. It was always a very lonely time. It had been seven years since Sarah had died and Christmas without a family of your own is nothing to write home about. It was always more of a burden than a delight - more to be dreaded than looked forward to. It was to be different this year, however.

First, I was looking forward to wearing my new gear. Roy and Pat had bought me a suit, two shirts, underwear, shoes and a tie for Christmas. As well as this some of the members of the church had clubbed together and bought me presents ranging from hair brushes and combs to fruit cakes. It was amazing and I was genuinely, deeply touched by it all.

Roy and Pat were especially kind and what they did for me must have been at great personal cost and sacrifice. They had three boys and a girl of their own and yet, under the Christmas tree in the living room, for every present belonging to a member of the family there was one for me.

I wasn't a member of their family and yet they made me feel like one. Through their kindness, feelings that had lain dormant in my heart for years were suddenly brought to the surface again. I was no longer a stranger and alone. I was once again part of a family - loved and cared for. Surely this is true Christian love in action!

I'm sure only eternity will reveal the impact and the outcome of the actions of those good and godly people. My own father had disowned me, but these people had taken me in as one of their own. It wasn't my fault that I was born illegitimate and was an embarrassment to my father, but I had done much worse by my own choice and yet these people were prepared to show me love. Surely, in heaven, they will have a great reward for helping to rescue one disillusioned and broken young man and doing something to restore his dignity.

"For as much as ye have done it unto one of the least of these, my brethren, ye have done it unto me." Surely those words of Jesus sum up the attitude and spirit of Roy and Pat Montgomery.

At the same time all of this illustrates the grace of a sovereign God and his unfailing provision. In spite of my hypocrisy he was still meeting my needs. I was finding out, through this, that God doesn't love us because of what we are. He loves us in spite of what we are.

I'm reminded of the account in John's gospel, chapter nineteen, of Christ's death on the cross. Just before he expired he turned to his mother and, referring to John said, "Woman, behold thy son." Then, turning to John he said of Mary, "Son, behold thy mother." The account concludes by telling us that from that time onwards John took Mary into his home. Even in his dying moments Jesus was making provision for his people.

And that immeasurable compassion still provides for the children of God today. I was an orphan, with no family. He provided a family in Roy and Pat. I had no home to go to on parole from prison. They opened up their home to me. If they hadn't done that I'd have spent yet another Christmas in the solitude of my cell.

Christmas morning in the Elim church was a lot different to what I had been used to. In fact, it wasn't like any other service I'd ever been to. The whole thing was very relaxed with the emphasis placed on the family. That was admirably demonstrated by the fact that there were children running about everywhere playing with their new toys.

There was no heavy theological sermon to have to try and digest before the turkey and plum pudding, just a couple of testimonies. These were brought by young men and were on the theme of Christmas and what it meant to them. Pastor McKee closed with a brief message on the theme of how precious Christmas would be if we but keep our eyes on the central character - Jesus.

The whole thing was beautiful, inspiring and well ordered. It gave me a great spiritual lift and brought home again to me the importance of that day, almost two thousand years ago, when God sent his son into the world to be born as a babe in Bethlehem.

In contrast, the rest of the day was spent as so many other people spend it, lazing about in front of the television set. However, it was just great to relax; to be away from the confined atmosphere of the prison; to be free from the sound of clanging doors and jangling keys, and not to have to jump at the barked orders of prison officers. This was the best Christmas I could remember!

But it was particularly memorable for another reason. The night before I went back into prison to conclude my sentence Roy and Pat and I again sat up for quite a while, just chatting. As before, Roy was on night shift with the taxi firm and had to leave for work around midnight. Pat and I sat on and continued our chat. As we talked she became very interested in spiritual matters. I had known for some time that she was convicted about her sin and that she recognised her need of Christ's salvation. But now she was prepared to face up to what she had to do - repent of her sin and receive Christ as her saviour.

It was a most wonderful moment when she and I knelt together and Pat, in a very simple but sincere way, asked the Lord Jesus into her heart. I have never known an experience like it. I think it can only be summed up in the words of the old Scottish saint who said of God's salvation, "It's better felt than telt." What a thrill to be there when someone is born into the family of God. No thrill this earth can offer could compare with it.

But lest you think this work of conversion in Pat's life was due to my ability or power, let me correct that notion. Salvation is all of grace. It is the work of God's Holy Spirit. It's the Holy Spirit who convicts of sin, who convinces of righteousness and who draws sinners to the Lord Jesus. We are only instruments in his hands. I had the privilege of leading Pat in the sinner's prayer. But there were many other links in the chain.

There was the faithful preaching of the gospel in the Elim church every week. There were the fervent prayers of many Christians in that church. And, also very important, there was the way Roy lived the Christian life before Pat and the children.

All this showed me how important each of us is in bringing others to the Saviour. God uses the smallest, most insignificant, things to do his work. And one of those things can be you or me. It's been my prayer that I'll always live to his glory and that others will always see Jesus in me. As Jesus said, "Let your light so shine before men that they may see your good works and glorify your father which is in heaven."

CHAPTER ELEVEN

THE FAMILY OF GOD

*"YE HAVE NOT RECEIVED THE SPIRIT OF BONDAGE AGAIN
TO FEAR; BUT YE HAVE RECEIVED THE SPIRIT OF ADOPTION
WHEREBY WE CRY ABBA, FATHER."*
ROMANS 8 v 15

My eventual release from Crumlin Road prison was on
the 10th February 1988. Naturally, for me, it couldn't come
quickly enough. After my parole, I became so impatient
and suffered what we refer to in prison as a severe dose of
'gate fever.'

When I stepped out onto the Crumlin Road and took my
first breath of freedom's air my faithful friend Roy Montgomery was there again to meet me. This time there was
less hurry in getting away from the place. I knew there was
no chance of them changing their minds and taking me back
inside. I had served my time. I had paid my debt to society.
Now, I was a free man! What a relief to know that I didn't
have to return - ever!

Once again Roy displayed his culinary skills when, at his
home, he presented me with a breakfast fit for a king. We
spent an hour or two catching up on what had been happening to us both since my last parole and Roy filled me in on
the latest news from the Elim church. Just then the church
pastor, Jackie McKee, arrived, with his wife, Kathleen.

They were laden down with boxes packed with every conceivable type of household utensil. There were pots and pans, delph, cutlery and bedclothes. In fact, everything except the kitchen sink. As they set them down on the floor Jackie explained.

"A few of the members got together and collected these things for you. You'll need them wherever you go to live. You'll need this too." With that he handed me an envelope and when I opened it there was £80 inside. This was also a gift from the church and was to help me start up a new life for myself. Pastor McKee also assured me that his help would be there anytime I needed it.

This was a great and pleasant surprise for me. The church had already been so good to me. Yet here they were expressing their Christian charity once again.

But the Lord had been good to me too. For, in reality, this was all his doing. He it was who had put it into their hearts to befriend a poor sinner. He it was who had laid upon their hearts a burden to pray for me while I was in prison. And now, he it was who had created for me a family in Ballysillan Elim church - a family I found I could rely on. I could only return him my heart felt thanks and praise his wonderful name.

During my last month in prison I had received a letter from an old friend who was also a landlord. He owned houses in East Belfast and he informed that he had a room for me in one of them, if I was interested. I certainly was very interested and replied immediately telling him so.

After my release I spent some time with Roy and Jackie, had a chat with them about my plans, thanked them for all the help they had been to me and then headed for east Belfast.

It was a big old house, on the Woodstock road, just opposite Willowfield police station and I had one room in it. It wasn't much of a place really and very small. At the time it seemed not much bigger than a shoe box. In fact it was actually smaller than a prison cell - and that's saying something. But at least I wasn't locked in for most of the day and with all it faults, I was thankful for it.

It was great to be out of prison and enjoying freedom at last. It was great to be able to attend church every week too. I went to Ballysillan Elim every Sunday and loved it. I had found a spiritual home there and had formed a good relationship with the other members. Now I had the chance to meet and have fellowship with a lot of the people who had been praying for me when I was in prison. Some of them were to become really close friends.

Jackie McKee, the pastor, and his wife were a tremendous source of help and encouragement. They counselled me in a number of personal matters and threw their home open to me at any time. They even gave me a bed for the night on one occasion when there was rioting in Belfast and they felt it was unwise for me to travel home across town.

Looking back I sometimes wonder how Jackie McKee put up with me and my persistent stubborness. I have long since lost count of the number of times we disagreed on theological matters. There were questions that I knew absolutely nothing about, yet I would argue and debate as if I was a long studied expert on them.

Thankfully, the evenings usually ended with Jackie putting his arm around my shoulder, correcting my error and pointing me in the right direction again. I always left Jackie's house a much wiser, and hopefully, more humble man.

Another young fellow who was to become a great friend of mine was Freddie McKeown. Freddie came from the Sunningdale area of Belfast and also attended Ballysillan Elim church.

He was, as they often say in evangelical circles, on fire for the Lord and I'm glad to say, some of this fire caught hold of me. Freddie loved to talk about the Lord, indeed it seems as if the Lord's name was never off his lips. This was so new to me. I had been used to men using the holy name frequently in the prison. But there it was in blasphemy and in vain. In Freddie's case it was in reverence and with great affection. The Lord was at work in his life and it was plain for everyone to see.

Over the months that we spent together Freddie taught me a lot. It wasn't just his knowledge of the scriptures or his ability to quote verses that impressed me, it was his faith too. He had a faith that was, on the one hand, simple and yet on the other, could move mountains. I remember the wonderful prayer times we had together. They were, as we often say, mighty and from them I gained a lot of strength.

As I've said before, the fact that I didn't have a family of my own made life tough for me. That was especially so at times like Christmas and birthdays. However, my first birthday after coming out of prison was totally different to anything I'd experienced for years.

It was coming up towards Easter and the church at Ballysillan had planned a fellowship tea - just a kind of a family get together. Freddie and I had tickets for it but, at the last minute, Freddie wasn't able to go and I was left to go on my own.

It was a superb supper consisting of a very well put together salad with all the trimmings, followed by the usual quota of cream cakes and biscuits. The whole evening was very enjoyable and there was plenty of fun too, with different members of the church getting up and making fools of themselves. Some performed mimes; some told jokes and some even ventured a song.

Towards the end of the evening Roger Abrol, the youth leader, made a fine speech thanking everyone for the organisation, the food provided and for coming - and then he dropped the bombshell.

"There's a brother here tonight who doesn't have a family of his own but we're very glad to have him as a member of our church family."

I didn't pay very much attention to this.

"And tonight's a very special one for this young man. It's his birthday!"

At this point I woke up with a start. The penny had finally dropped.

"Let's all sing 'Happy birthday,' to brother Graham Lawther," Roger continued and then he started them off.

Well I sat there flabbergasted as the whole assembly burst into song - for me. I hadn't expected anything like this. I didn't even realise anyone knew it was my birthday. But I can tell you I sure was chuffed by it all. And it didn't end there.

When the singing stopped someone turned down the lights and from the back of the church Kathleen, the pastor's wife, appeared carrying a great big birthday cake, festooned with candles all burning like little lamps. Kathleen walked right over to where I sat, plonked the cake down in front of me and told me to blow out the candles. I could hardly see them for the tears in my eyes but I managed it just the same.

After blowing out the candles, Pastor McKee asked me to come to the front of the church and give my testimony. He introduced me by saying that I was to be baptized the following night, Sunday, but that it would be a good idea if just now I took five minutes to share some of my personal circumstances with them.

Nothing like this had happened to me since I had been a child and I was completely choked up with emotion over the whole thing. But it was a great experience and a wonderful gesture from those lovely people in Ballysillan. It wasn't just that they gave me a birthday cake. It was more than that. These people, through their kindness and thoughtfulness, had given me a sense of belonging; a sense of security and identity. I was now among the people of God, a people who loved me, cared for me and made me feel at home. It was a great privilege for me to be counted as one of them.

The following day was Easter Sunday and all day long I looked forward to the evening church service. Baptismal services in evangelical circles are rather special events, usually very well attended and often quite emotional.

A lot of people had told me about their baptism experiences. It seemed to me that each of them could remember it as if it were yesterday. They still spoke about it with great enthusiasm and told me it would be an experience of a lifetime, one I would never forget.

Although I had made the decision to be baptised I still didn't fully understand the spiritual significance of it. Another believer explained it to me like this.

"This, Graham, is really your opportunity to make a public profession of Jesus Christ as your Saviour. I suppose it's a bit like two people who fall in love and want to get married."

"On a beautiful, moonlit autumn night they both stand looking over a five barred gate into a field of golden corn wafting in the gentle breeze. Romance is in the air and Johnny, overcome by the beauty of the occasion, finally manages to say what's been in his heart for weeks.

'Mary, will you marry me?' he whispers softly.

"Far from being taken aback by this sudden expression of Johnny's admiration for her, Mary replies, after a careful and calculated pause, 'Yes Johnny, I will marry you.'

"But Graham, that's not the end of the matter. They don't just run off and set up home together from that moment on. Mary says, 'We'll have to go public on this Johnny. There'll have to be a wedding service.' And of course Johnny, being an honourable chap, agrees."

"Now Graham, that's just like our conversion to Christ. At conversion we're united to him in heart and in faith and from that moment our lives are changed, or they should be. From the moment of conversion we are one with him and it's from that moment that we begin to walk in the newness of life spoken of in Romans Ch. 6 verse 4."

"Baptism is more like the actual wedding ceremony. At the wedding Mary and Johnny declare publicly the intentions they have already pledged in private. They want the whole world to know that they are one with each other and so they make their vows public."

"And at baptism that's what we, as believers, are doing. We are saying, 'I have turned away from sin and self and personal ambition. I have identified myself with Christ and his death on the cross. I too have died to self and am now one with Jesus Christ. His way is now my way. His will is now my will. I intend to serve him with all I have for the rest of my life.'"

I had never seen so many people in the church as on the night of that baptismal service. It was absolutely packed to capacity.

After the gospel service, the ten of us who were to be baptised assembled at the front of the church. The baptismal was already filled with water and one by one we were invited to give brief testimony to our salvation. Then, stepping down into the pool, where the pastor and another elder were waiting, we were each baptised.

As I stood there, waist deep in water, Pastor McKee said to me, "Brother Graham, on profession of your faith in the Lord Jesus Christ, I baptise you in the name of the Father and of the Son and of the Holy Ghost. Amen."

Then he lowered me under the water and helped me up again. As I climbed back up the steps, out of the pool, a great sense of peace flooded my heart. It was a very emotional experience and there and then I resolved afresh to follow my Lord wherever he would lead me.

CHAPTER 12

THROUGH MANY TRIALS!

"THINK IT NOT STRANGE CONCERNING THE FIERY TRIAL WHICH IS TO TRY YOU."
I PETER 4:12

In the immediate weeks after my release from prison life for me went quite well - apart from the boredom. I had chosen to live in East Belfast. That meant that, during the week, I was isolated from the friends I saw at week-ends. Most of them lived in the Ballysillan area, near the church, and the only time I got to see them was at the Sunday services. A few hours of fellowship once a week was hardly enough.

It's not surprising, then, that it wasn't long before I became very lazy and found petty excuses for not attending the meetings. The simple consequence of this was that I felt more and more lonely and that old enemy, depression, returned to haunt me. All my great enthusiasm evaporated and like Samson, sheared of his locks, my spiritual strength vanished.

However, there was another problem too. There was a very ungodly environment in the house which I shared. There were six other residents there, all of them quite fond of a drink. At the week-ends they held rather wild parties which went on into the early hours of the next day. It was sometimes three o'clock on a Sunday morning before the music, loud and disturbing, eventually stopped and sleep could be attempted.

I used to really hate the racket they made. It was so frustrating lying there, listening to that rumpus and unable to sleep, especially when I had to rise so early next morning for church. When I think about it now I realize it was no place for a young convert like me.

At that time I was doing voluntary work for an organisation called CHRISTIAN CHARITABLE VOLUNTARY HELPS. It had been set up by a local businessman, Tommy Coey, who loved the Lord and wanted to give assistance to people who were deprived of the basic necessities of life. He got the use of an old factory, in the Newtownards Road area, which he renovated and turned into a day care shelter.

I worked for him as the project leader, looking after the basic running of the place, collecting monies and subscriptions and making sure that everybody had whatever they needed.

This left Tommy, who was a self employed chef, to get on with his own work and thus raise money to fund the project. Tommy Coey is a lovely man and during all the time I was there he treated me like his own son. We had a very close relationship and I can honestly say that I loved him in the Lord. In all the time I worked with him he had only one goal in life and that was to reach men and women with the gospel of Christ. It's still my prayer that God will prosper everything he puts his hand to for the kingdom of God.

One evening, when I arrived home from the centre, the most startling news awaited me. Danny, one of the other lads who lived in the place, came into the living room with the message.

"Graham, there was a probation officer here today looking for you. He slipped a note under your door."

I dashed up stairs to my room, anxious to know what, if anything, could be the matter. Since my release from prison I had been walking the line. I hadn't put a foot out of place. My life had been lived by the book, as far as the law was concerned. Why would a probation officer be looking for me?

I picked up the note and with hands trembling, read it. Imagine my surprise when I discovered that I had become a father! The simple message read, "You have a healthy baby girl and the mother would like to see you." At the bottom of the note the probation officer had written his name and telephone number and included a P.S. "If you have any problems, contact me."

Before I had gone to jail I had been keeping company with a girl from the other side of Belfast. I didn't even realise that she was expecting a baby, or that I was to be a father, but now that I was confronted with the situation I would have to face it like a man.

Actually, my first reaction was one of overwhelming joy. Me! A father! I couldn't believe it! Yet I never doubted that it was true.

Eventually, I was able to visit the mother and see the child. I suppose, like every father and mother, I thought she was just beautiful. So tiny. So innocent. And - so helpless.

"This little one," I thought, "must be cared for. She must be loved and provided for. She must not be deserted by her father, as I was." I was resolved that I would do everything I could to give this little daughter of mine all the things I had been deprived of.

But, "the best laid schemes o' mice and men," and all that. The good relationship between the mother and me soon dissolved. We fell out and that put an end to me seeing the child any more.

There was another rather serious problem which made the situation even worse. This girl was a Roman Catholic and lived in the New Lodge road area of the city. Since I was an ex UVF man and had spent time in 'A' wing of Crumlin prison, where republican prisoners saw me and could identify me as being from a loyalist background, it wasn't very wise for me to be regularly going to this girl's house.

As well as this I had to be careful about loyalists seeing me going into that area. They may have concluded that I was some kind of informer to the republican movement. The consequences of that are all too evident in the streets of Belfast, week by week. I'm no coward but there's no way I wanted to end up another statistic in the Northern Ireland casualty figures.

In the light of all this I decided not to pursue the matter of seeing the child but just to make it a matter of prayer and leave the initiative to the girl.

Although the girl never gave me any reason for our fall out I'm pretty sure I know what the problem was. I was now a Christian and doing my best to serve God, albeit in a struggling manner. She didn't share my beliefs or my desire to please God. That left us poles apart spiritually, and with neither of us willing to make changes, there was really no option but to go our separate ways.

All this didn't alter the fact that I still loved that little child and wanted to do everything possible to provide for her. Even after our parting I wrote to the mother several times, enquiring about the child and wishing the mother well too. But I can't remember ever getting a reply, that is until one fateful day. But I'll come back to that later.

It's a strange thing to have to say but one which will be backed up by many other people involved in full time christian work. You often get as much opposition from within the church as you do from without. Didn't Jesus say,

"A man's foes shall be those of his own household." It's an awful pity that this is so, for manys a good, sincere man or woman, with a genuine burden for the souls of men and a desire to extend the kingdom of God, has either been forced out of the Lord's work or just given up the battle, simply because of the criticism or fault finding of people who should, but obviously, don't know better.

A man doesn't dot the eyes and stroke the tees as they think they should be dotted and stroked and so they mount some kind of insidious campaign to make his life difficult or impossible. Sometimes the opposition is quite open and face to face. Other times it's more subtle and underhand; scheming and plotting, sometimes for years until they achieve their pernicious goal - the downfall of a servant of God.

But either way it's totally wrong and completely contrary to the teaching of scripture where we are exhorted to, "bear one another's burdens and so fulfil the law of Christ;" - "restore those overtaken by a fault;" - and to, "let brotherly love continue."

I say all this just to encourage any other young person who may be contemplating any kind of Christian service, whether full or part time. I say it also, to warn them of the pitfalls and attitudes that can, at the very least, weaken their effectiveness for the Lord and may possibly destroy their prospects entirely.

As I write this there comes to mind one incident in my early Christian service that should have been a lesson to me, but in hindsight, wasn't.

A man called Eric Lennon came to see me one day at the CHRISTIAN CHARITY VOLUNTARY HELPS office. Eric is a Christian author and at the time was also director of the well known, Shankill Road Mission.

He came to see me with a view to offering me some form of ministry with the mission. However, I'm afraid to have to report that his visit that day was a complete waste of his time. No matter which way he approached the subject he couldn't get any measure of co-operation from me. Eventually, he left with the opinion, and he was probably quite correct, that I was a pompous, big headed, know it all. Eric left and I suppose should never have approached me about Christian service again. However, in the process of time, as it will be become clear later in this book, he did and I have a lot to be grateful to him for. Nowadays he's a man that I have a high regard for.

As well as working at C.C.V.H. I was also out and about different churches, addressing meetings, giving my testimony and gaining valuable experience in public speaking.

After a short time an invitation came from John Duncan, the director of Youth for Christ, Northern Ireland. He asked if I'd give my testimony at a Youth for Christ rally in the Ulster Hall.

Well, as you can probably imagine, I was very excited about this and couldn't wait to tell Tommy Coey. He was just as excited and suggested that, at the meeting, I wear a sweatshirt with the motto, "C.C.V.H. HELPS," emblazoned in black letters on the front of it. I thought this was a great idea although, looking back now, I'm not so sure. In some ways it seems to cheapen, even commercialise the gospel. But that's just by the way; and it's only my notion. I'm sure there may be perfectly good reasons, some times, for advertising a particular branch of the Lord's work.

Anyway, on the night of the meeting I made my way along to the Ulster Hall in good time. I wanted to get settled before the meeting started and if possible, have a preliminary chat with John Duncan.

When I arrived in down town Belfast and turned the corner into Bedford Street I got the surprise of my life. It was still an hour and a half before the meeting was due to start but already there was a queue of over a thousand people.

I felt myself go weak at the knees. The biggest crowd I had ever faced had been in the Elim church at Ballysillan - and I had been nervous there. This crowd frightened me. By the time we all sat on the Ulster Hall stage and looked at the sea of faces that lay before us I was near enough terrified. The Ulster Hall was packed to capacity. Someone said there were over two thousand people there, with about a hundred more turned away. There just wasn't any more room. I had never seen so many people in the one place, at the one time, praising God. And when they stood to sing the opening hymn, it was like a foretaste of Heaven.

I dreaded the possibility of making a fool of myself before such a massive crowd. But I needn't have worried. They were gracious and sympathetic in the extreme. They listened attentively, laughed at my jokes, and when I sometimes got it wrong by holding the microphone too far away, so they couldn't hear properly, they were patient. And when I eventually got it right again, they applauded. They were a super crowd and really made me feel at home.

The testimony was brief. John had given me a time limit of about twelve minutes because they were working to a fairly tight schedule. Afterwards, when I sat down, I thought.

"What a tremendous experience! A lad like me giving my testimony in a place like this, and to such a crowd."

•••••••

I remember a Christian once telling me that as soon a you make any effort to serve God the Devil will be on the warpath. He'll be just around the corner waiting to pounce and if possible, to destroy you. Shortly after the big Ulster

Hall rally I was to discover just how true that is and it brings me back to that relationship with the girl from the New Lodge Road.

I was sitting one afternoon in the upstairs room of my shared house in East Belfast, quietly studying my Bible, when a knock came to the front door. After a few moments I heard the door being opened and the muffled sound of voices as a brief conversation took place. Then the door closed again and the caller, apparently satisfied, left.

But the door was hardly shut till I heard the heavy sound of footsteps coming up the stairs and then a fist banging on my door. When I opened it two of the other lads who lived in the house stood there, almost breathless.

"Graham," they blurted the words out, "the cops were here looking for you but we told them you weren't in."

"Why did you do that," I retorted. "I've done nothing and I've nothing to hide."

"Well we weren't sure," they replied. "We thought that perhaps you were in some trouble again and we'd better give you some time to cover your tracks."

Well I suppose they had acted in my best interests but still, I didn't have anything to hide and I couldn't go around looking over my shoulder all the time, so I decided to go down to the police station and see what they wanted.

The desk sergeant in Willowfield R.U.C. station had a lot to learn about diplomacy and tact, I thought. When I first approached him and asked if the police wanted to see me, he asked my name. After I had told him and he was now sure that he was speaking to the right person he said,

"You're that young fellow from across the street. North Queen Street barracks were on to us about you. Something to do with some child dying. They asked us to get in touch with you and let you know."

What a way to hear about my little daughter's death! Had this man no sensitivity or compassion at all? Which school of diplomacy had he attended? He might not have known that I was the child's father, although I felt that he should, but surely he could have taken me aside privately and broken the news a bit more gently. As it was, he just told me straight out, standing there in the public enquiries office of a police station. The tragic news was broken to me as if my daughter was a total stranger, and not my own flesh and blood.

By the time I got to the flat on the New Lodge Road the mother was in a state of shock. The doctor had already been with her and had given her something to calm her but she was still in a terrible state, as I'm sure you'll appreciate.

One of her friends spotted me and recognising that I was a stranger, realized I must be the child's father. She expressed her sympathy and then went on to explain what had happened. The child had died during the night, quite suddenly, in what is commonly referred to as a cot death, now more properly known as sudden infant death.

I managed to spend a few moments with my former girl friend in an effort to console her in her grief, but I might as well not have been there. She was so completely absorbed in the tragedy of the child's death that everyone else around her didn't matter. She sat there in total silence - heartbroken.

I decided it would be better all round if I left for a while in the hope that even a short space of time would allow some healing to take place. Shortly after I came back the undertaker arrived on the scene and proceeded with his unenviable task of laying out the little infant in her tiny white coffin. I must say that he performed his duties with the utmost compassion and sympathy and was anxious to do whatever he could to ease the pain that was breaking the mother's heart.

The death of a child must be one of the most harrowing experiences a parent can ever be faced with. It seems so needless and so pointless. As I looked at my daughter lying there in that little casket, so innocent and for all the world like a doll, I couldn't help wishing that, somehow, the hands of time could be turned back. If they could I was sure she would never have been conceived.

Yet, it must be remembered that God makes no mistakes. He alone is the author of life and He had given this little one life, if only for a spell. If we believe in a sovereign God we must accept that He must have had some purpose in it, even though, for the moment, we can't see it.

One thing, above all others, bothered me that evening. It was the discussion which took place as to whether or not a candle should be lit for the child. I'm not exactly sure about the significance of lighting a candle when someone dies. Some say it's to show the soul the way to heaven. Some, that's it's to ward off evil spirits; and others that it's to indicate the continuation of eternal life after physical death.

Whatever the reason, I was convinced there was no need for it. I was certain that this child of mine was with the Lord and that all the candles ever burned would make no difference to her eternal destiny. That had been settled, two thousand years ago, by the death of Christ. Even though she had not come to the age of understanding and into a personal relationship with Jesus, His precious blood had been shed for her, as for all mankind, therefore I would see her, some day, in Heaven.

How I hope and pray that God will open the eyes of all those, blinded by the notion of human ritual, to see that in Christ and in Christ alone, there is forgiveness of sin, peace with God and an entrance to Heaven.

Two days later, on a Saturday morning, the child's funeral took place. The burial was at Milltown cemetery on the Falls Road, the very heart of republican West Belfast.

The first part of the funeral proceedings was held in the mother's home, and included a Roman Catholic service. I wasn't very impressed by what the priest had to say, nor by the rituals he performed. It all seemed to consist more of superstition than of what the Bible teaches. But I had to be there and I had to endure it. There was nothing I could say at that point. My moment, hopefully, would come later.

The most difficult moment, however, came when it fell to me to place the lid on that little white coffin and close the light of this world away from her sweet little face, forever.

It was made worse by the fact that, at this juncture, the child's mother went into complete hysterics. I suppose the realisation that she would never see her little girl again was finally too much for her and she just fell to pieces.

Only a small number of mourners, about fifteen, went the whole way to the cemetery. Throughout the journey I sat in the back of the car and nursed the tiny coffin across my knees. It was a harrowing experience and during every yard of the journey I could only wish that, somehow, I could be spirited away from this heartbreaking situation.

When we arrived at Milltown cemetery the parish priest was already there and making his preparations for the burial. What took place there was all new to me. The priest stood there reading from a small black book, pausing every so often, at which point those around the grave responded by chanting something which sounded like a prayer to the virgin Mary.

Eventually, the priest sprinkled some of his 'holy water' over the coffin before the grave diggers slowly lowered it into the ground.

As soon as the service was over and as the mourners stood around offering sympathy, I went over and thanked the priest for his attention and presented him with a copy of, 'The Christian Workers New Testament.'

For those readers who are not familiar with, 'The Christian Workers New Testament,' I should explain that, throughout the book, there are a number of verses which are underlined in red ink. These take the reader, step by step, through the plan of salvation - pointing out that man is a sinner; that Christ died for his sins and that salvation is free through what Christ has accomplished on the Cross.

The priest took the book from me and flicked through the pages noticing the verses underlined in red. He asked me what they meant and I did my best to explain their purpose to him. I followed it up with a brief account of my own experience of God's salvation. The simplest way to record the priest's reaction to all this is to say that he was dumbstruck. Absolutely dumbstruck. I suppose the poor man had never come across the like before.

CHAPTER THIRTEEN

WHEN GOD REBUKES HIS CHILD

"AS MANY AS I LOVE I REBUKE AND CHASTEN."
REVELATION 3 v 19.

The death of the child and the heart breaking circumstances surrounding her funeral were not the end of this sorry chapter in my life. What happened back in my former girlfriend's flat, after the funeral, almost upstaged all of that.

One by one the mourners and relatives left the flat and eventually, the girl and I were left alone. She was still visibly shaken by the whole thing, didn't want to talk about it and was completely withdrawn. However, dejected as she was, I didn't expect what followed next. In fact it took me completely by surprise.

She made what appeared to be a routine visit to the bathroom but while she was there, proceeded to make what turned out to be a very serious attempt on her own life.

First, she swallowed the remaining contents of a bottle of sleeping pills and then, with a razor blade, slashed the inside of her forearms from elbow to wrist. To make the plan even more successful, and to avoid arousing suspicion in me, she then came back into the living room and snuggled into a sleeping bag which lay on the sofa, tucking her arms inside the bag.

All the while I had been with her since after the funeral she had been repeating over and over again, "I want to be with my baby." I suppose her plan was to lie there and allow the life to slowly drain from her. The tragic thing is, if her plan had been allowed to succeed, instead of seeing her baby which was now in God's presence, she would have suffered not only the loss of her life but the loss of her soul forever. Such is the wicked power Satan wields over the hearts of us poor mortals in our unregenerate state.

Thinking back on the events of that night the speed of my reaction to what she had done surprised even me. Despite her efforts to cover up the wounds some of the blood, which was literally pouring from her body, dripped onto the floor and I spotted it. As soon as I discovered what she had done I tore a pillowslip into bandages and quickly wrapped them around her bleeding arms.

The first aid completed, I dashed upstairs to the next flat and hammered on the door until the fellow inside answered. he could hardly understand me as I babbled out the problem, but eventually, I managed to persuade him to dial 999 and call an ambulance.

The ambulance dashed straight to the Mater hospital on the Crumlin Road and the patient was rushed straight through to casualty where a doctor and medical team were awaiting her arrival. Meanwhile I had to suffer the further frustration of standing at the reception desk and filling out all the necessary forms.

The other people in reception stared at me in astonishment. I could fully understand why. I looked more like a soldier just returned from the front line of a war. My hair was tossed, my face had a sickly pallor through lack of sleep, my whole appearance was dishevelled and my suit was soaked with blood. To put it mildly, I was a sorry sight!

As I stood there, a dreadful mess, the doctor came to ask for some information about her. What sort of tablets had she taken, and how many? Had she ever tried this sort of thing before? Was there anyone to look after her if she was allowed home?

I had taken the medicine bottle with me to the hospital and was able to tell him approximately how many tablets she had swallowed. She certainly had never done anything like this before, to my knowledge, but then she had never been faced with a situation like this before.

The doctor was satisfied that there was no immediate risk to her life but decided that it would be best if she could be kept in hospital for a while. It took quite sometime to patch her up, she needed forty stitches in her arms, but when they had finished she absolutely refused to stay in the place.

Well of course, the doctor wouldn't hear tell of this and after a bit of wrangling and dealing asked if I could help. I offered to bring her home to my place and to give her my bed while I slept on the floor. To my surprise she agreed.

I realised that bringing this former girlfriend, and the mother of our dead child, home to my flat wasn't the wisest of moves. It certainly went against my better judgment. All that had taken place over the past few days had left me in a state of emotional confusion so I was in no fit state to look after someone who was so depressed and suicidal. I could hardly look after myself.

However, I felt obligated to do whatever I could to help her in her hour of need. And maybe I felt just a little bit guilty too. After all, hadn't I been instrumental in landing her in this situation? I didn't really have any option but to help her.

Over the next few days a constant stream of doctors and district nurses called at the house to check up on the patient. Eventually, one of them decided that a spell in psychiatric care would do her good and a letter admitting her to

127

Purdysburn Hospital, on the outskirts of Belfast, was issued.

However, admission was entirely voluntary and she stayed only one day before insisting on coming home with me again. As soon as she telephoned me I went to Purdysburn and collected her. This was a serious mistake on my part, for really she was in need of proper hospital care. I would venture to say it was a mistake on the part of the medical profession too. The doctors should have insisted on her being hospitalised. It shouldn't have been left to her to decide. She was in no fit state to do that.

Furthermore, her presence in my flat wasn't doing me any good either. The strain of trying to look after her was proving too much for me - I could no longer cope. In fact, if it hadn't been for the assistance of two stalwart friends I'm sure I would have completely cracked up and ended up in Purdysburn myself.

However, the Lord always sends along the right help at the right time! David Edwards and Bobby Lewis were both elders in Spamount Congregational Church. Both of them, plus a few of their friends, rallied round me at this time of crisis and pulled me through. They drove me wherever I needed to go, advised me on what plan of action to follow and of course, supported me with their prayers. Without them I don't think I would have been able to cope.

Sometimes people say that the family of God isn't what it used to be. It comes under a lot of criticism from a lot of people who really should know better. They say that there's not the same charity and compassion as there was years ago. But I can only speak from my experience. A lot of Christian people have given me a lot of help. They have given me help which has cost them financially and practically. I want to say thank you to them all. As far as I'm concerned the family of God is the most precious thing on earth.

It has to be said that it was the friendship of God's people and their fervent prayers on my behalf which brought me through this present crisis too. All the recent events shook me to my spiritual foundations and when they had finished shaking me, the foundations were all I had left. That deep depression descended, like a black cloud, again. The Bible was cast aside. Church attendance ceased - and prayer went by the wall. But for the mercy and grace of God, I believe Satan would have succeeded in provoking me to suicide.

I suppose some people will be critical at this point and accuse me of being a spiritual weakling, unable to face any hurdle I came to. Well, in a way, they're right. I was a spiritual weakling. But remember, I was still just a spiritual infant; barely a toddler in Christian terms. Nobody expects a toddler to have the strength and intellect of a man in the physical world. Why should they expect it in the spiritual?

And just while I'm on this point. How many Christians have been through what I've through in their entire Christian life, let alone in the first months after coming to Christ? I'm not proud of what has happened to me. I often wish it had never taken place. But at the same time I'm painting the picture, warts and all, and giving God the glory for my deliverance.

As I have said, that deliverance came through the prayers of faithful christians.

Davy Edwards was a student at Belfast Bible College. He reported my misfortunes to the students and staff there and every morning, at their devotions, my case was upheld at the throne of grace. He told them, too, of the zeal I once had and claimed that God still had a work for me to do.

Up at Ballysillan Elim church the members were still faithfully remembering me too. In fact, they had never ceased to do so. Unknown to me at the time there was one particular evening, at a midweek service, when Roy Montgomery and Freddie McKeown had been particularly burdened to pray for me. Even though I hadn't seen them in months, that night they specifically asked the Lord to bring me back into their fellowship. They loved me in the Lord, they felt I belonged there and believed they could care for me.

Their prayers were answered sooner then even they could have expected. That night, as in the past few nights, I found it impossible to sleep. At three o'clock in the morning I was so distressed that I telephoned Pastor Jackie McKee to ask him if he could see me as soon as possible. Of course, being the man he is, he agreed to meet me the very next morning.

However, I didn't wait for Pastor McKee to come to me. The next morning I was up before dawn and walked the whole way from East Belfast to Ballysillan, a distance of about three miles, to the home of Roy and Pat Montgomery.

Even though it was not yet seven o'clock Roy and Pat were delighted to see me. They brought me in and immediately began to pamper me. It wasn't long before I was tucking into another of Roy's great breakfasts, with a runny egg and a mug of hot tea. Then the talking began in earnest.

Roy assured me that despite what had happened in the past three months God still loved me. No matter how I had let the Lord down there was still forgiveness. And no matter how inconsistent I had been there was still another chance.

Roy and Pat also invited me to come and stay with them - for as long as I needed to. That came as a great relief to me and I accepted immediately.

Even though I had prayed the sinner's prayer again and longed to do what was right in God's sight, for the first week or so that I was there, I didn't feel the sense of peace and forgiveness that I longed for. However, one morning as I was walking past the Bilston Road Mission Hall, praying as usual for forgiveness and peace, the text on their notice board caught my eye. It was from Isaiah chapter one and it read,

"Though your sins be as scarlet they shall be as white as snow; though they be red like crimson, they shall be as wool."

That verse from God's word came to my heart like a balm. For the first time since my daughter had died, peace was restored to my heart and the God shaped vacuum in my life filled up again. As I walked on, another verse from the Bible came to mind. It was from the book of Judges and the story of Samson. During her attempts to beguile Samson, Delilah used these words and now, even though they were taken out of context with the story, God used them to speak to me. After a number of unsuccessful attempts to find out the secret of Samson's strength, Delilah implored, "How can you say, 'I love you, when your heart is not with me?"

Now God was saying something like that to me. That still, small voice seemed to say, "You say that you love me. Why don't you prove it by living right?"

From that moment, as I walked onward, my step was lighter, my heart was merrier and my soul was free! God had forgiven me as soon as I had asked him to, but now I felt it within - and that made all the difference. Oh I know that feelings aren't everything - and they're seldom to be trusted - but at the same time it makes all the difference to feel God at work in your life.

At the same time I think it's true to say that God was teaching me another lesson - the lesson of humility. Pride is a great sin and particularly destructive, especially in one who aspires to serve the Lord. It must be eradicated if a life of service is to be fruitful. Perhaps the Lord, in his great wisdom, had allowed me to fall, just to let me see how hopeless I was on my own.

However, there's another good side to this learning process. If you've never fallen yourself you don't what it feels like. On the other hand if, like me, you've had a number of tumbles then you can sympathise - yea empathise, with others who fall. I think that I can do that now - and do it very well. One of the great fruits of humility is compassion for others. I hope, after all that's happened to me, I have, at least, a measure of Christian compassion.

CHAPTER FOURTEEN

SETTLING IN

"BUT THOU ISRAEL, AR MY SERVANT."
ISAIAH 41 v 8.

Living with Roy and Pat Montgomery was wonderful and I was very grateful to them for their kindness. However, it could only be a temporary measure. I couldn't impose on their generosity indefinitely. I couldn't go back to East Belfast either. The circumstances there were far from ideal. Besides, I wanted to attend the church at Ballysillan regularly and I could only do that if I had somewhere fairly convenient to there to live.

I suppose I could have approached the Housing Executive again, but the thought of going on a long waiting list quickly put me off the idea. The Housing Executive allocate their houses on a points system. Obviously, someone with a wife and young children is in much more need of a place to live than a single man, so it may have taken at least three months to house me and that, short though it may seem to some, was far too long to have to wait.

Private landlords were also a non-starter. Comparable accommodation would cost much more than the Housing

Executive would charge and I just couldn't afford it.

After I had spent about three weeks in Roy's house I decided to give the homeless advice centre, in Bedford Street, a call. Maybe they could do something.

It was a Friday afternoon when I dropped into their office and after hanging around for quite a while, I was called to the enquiry desk.

There were the usual questions to be answered and forms to be filled out. I did my best to impress upon the young lady the urgency of my case, although, I suppose everybody does that. She was quite pleasant and said that my application would be sent off to the Executive by internal mail. That would speed things a bit, at least. I asked if that was the only way the form could be delivered and she replied that, if I wanted to, I could take it round there myself.

The Housing Executive's offices are right in the centre of Belfast, in Royal Avenue. I grabbed the form and hurried round there as quickly as I could, praying all the way that God would do something special for me.

When I got there, just before they closed the doors, the place was empty. That meant no queuing anyway, so I walked straight to the counter and presented my application to the receptionist. As she stood there checking the form and making sure that all the details had been given I asked how long it would take before I could be allocated a house.

"It will take between ten days and two weeks before we can assess your points value. It's really anyone's guess after that. It just depends on what's available."

"I haven't got all that time," I replied, somewhat in despair. "I need somewhere right now!"

I stepped out onto the busy streets of Belfast again with an anxious heart. What I'd just been told made the picture look rather bleak, but then, somehow my faith shone through. I felt compelled to pray and there, as the teeming crowds on Royal Avenue jostled to and fro on that Friday afternoon, I lifted my heart to God.

"Lord," I said out loud, "I know that nothing is impossible to you. No matter what anybody says you can get me a place to live. Please get me somewhere soon!"

Although I had no idea what the future held, as I stood there alone in that crowed Belfast street, I felt content. God had heard my cry. Surely he would intervene.

Well it was only three working days later, on Wednesday morning, that the Lord answered my prayer. He had speeded up, or short circuited, all the red tape and administration procedures and in that short space of time had provided me with a two bedroom, semi-detached house in the Silverstream Estate, in North Belfast.

It was less than one hundred yards from where Roy and Pat Montgomery lived and within easy walking distance of the church. As well as that, quite a few of my Christian friends lived in the area too.

I felt like the man in the Bible who was blind from birth. When Jesus restored his sight, all his friends, and a few critics too, wanted to know how this impossible thing had happened. They demanded to know just how the miracle had been performed. The man's answer is, as we say in Belfast, choice.

"All I know is, a man called Jesus, made clay and anointed my eyes and said to me , 'Go and wash them in the pool of Siloam,' and when I did so, I could see."

That man hadn't a clue how Jesus restored his sight but he sure enjoyed being able to see. I was exactly the same. I didn't know how God got me the house so quickly but it didn't stop me moving in. I had prayed and the Lord had exceeded my wildest expectations.

I turned the key in the door and stepped into that house with tear filled eyes. I couldn't contain the joy that welled up in my heart. The house was perfect, except for one thing.

There wasn't a stick of furniture in it. So I just prayed again. And would you believe it, within two weeks that house was completely furnished with everything I needed. The Lord brought different believers my way, all with something that I needed for my new house. One brought a bed, another brought a suite of furniture and yet another brought a cooker.

It was truly amazing how the Lord brought them all together and it was even more amazing how the various items matched. There were no colour clashes. The living room suite and the curtains for the windows came from total strangers, but they matched perfectly. I know it sounds incredible, too good to be true but why shouldn't it happen and why shouldn't his young servant have a modicum of comfort.

A lot of people would be quite content to palm off the Lord's people with second best, indeed with any old thing. If perchance you're one of them may I very gently remind you of a story I once heard about Charles Haddon Spurgeon, the great Baptist preacher who lived during the last century.

He was travelling on the train one day and he met another of the Lord's servants. This man appeared to have more than a touch of that introverted pride that some people are cursed with.

This man said, "I'm travelling third class and saving the Lord's money." I think by this he meant to gently chide Mr. Spurgeon. But the great man replied, quick as a flash and with perhaps just a hint of sarcasm, "I'm travelling first class - and saving the Lord's servant."

During all this time the Lord had been working in my heart in a powerful way. My faith was now stronger than it had ever been. I had been broken and remade or, to change the metaphor, led out of by-path meadow onto the straight and narrow way again.

One of the many victories that I was particularly thankful for was the deliverance from cigarette smoking. For thirteen and a half years I had been totally enslaved by the habit and try as I might, I just couldn't break its power. As a christian it used to embarrass me that I couldn't rid myself of such a filthy habit.

However, one Sunday evening I sat listening to a tape by the great Ulster preacher and evangelist, W.P. Nicholson. He was preaching on the unpardonable sin, which incidentally, isn't smoking, or drinking, or any of the other things that people normally associate with the ungodly. In fact, the unpardonable sin, briefly explained, is the final rejection of the witness of the Holy Spirit to the saving work of Christ. That is the only sin which God cannot and will not pardon. All other sins, however great, can and will be pardoned through Christ's death on the cross.

However, as I listened to Mr. Nicholson's message the Holy Spirit arrested me, so much so, that I shook from within. It seemed as though my whole body was covered in goose pimples and the hairs on the back of my neck stood out straight.

As the words of that God anointed man came from the loudspeaker the fear of a Christless eternity gripped me. The Holy Spirit brought all the inconsistencies of the past eighteen months of my christian experience before me. He showed me what a spiritual failure I was and how Christ had gone to the cross and died for me. Yet I couldn't even give up something as simple as smoking - for him.

I had been telling lots of people how the Lord had changed my life and yet, where was the evidence of this change? Was I not still doing many things that were an affront to him and a hindrance to my testimony?

The real crunch came when Mr. Nicholson said, "There is a fine line between grace and damnation and once a man crosses that line there is no turning back - ever!"

"Once a man crosses that fatal line," the voice continued, "All fear of God is gone and like Cane, in the Old Testament, he is left to wander in spiritual darkness and is marked until the day of judgment."

These truths smote home to my heart like the arrow from the marksman's bow. Under irresistible conviction from the Holy Spirit I cried out to God for mercy. In fact I didn't just cry, I begged. On my knees I pleaded with God to come into my heart afresh and to help me live for him.

That night I placed my all on the altar and asked God to take my broken life and do something with that would bring him glory. From that moment there was a new Graham Lawther - the old one was no more.

There was a new attitude too. Gone was the hardness, the spiritual pride, the arrogance and the pig headedness. In its place there was gentleness, meekness and a willingness to learn. After months and years of striving and struggling I finally realised that I was nothing more than a poor sinner, saved by grace, who could do nothing without God's help.

The house and all its furnishings were not the only blessings God was to shower upon me. Within another month or so he provided me with a job also.

In Northern Ireland there's a government jobs scheme entitled Action for Community Employment - ACE for short. It's government funded and basically its aim is to provide training and jobs for the long term unemployed. Originally the work was community orientated but that has become less of a restriction in recent years.

Pastor Jackie McKee had plans to set up a job advice centre in the Ballysillan area and asked me if I'd be interested in becoming the supervisor. He suggested that I go down town to the job centre and fill in the necessary application forms.

Some six weeks later I started work with the grand, imposing title of job advice officer. The only problem, and this is the laughable bit, there was no one for me to advise. The scheme didn't yet have offices and with no offices there could be no applicants.

Jackie McKee had his eye on an old three story building that used to be the depot for a taxi firm. It was owned by a local publican and my first job was to go along to him and make a bid on the place. I was given a figure of two thousand pounds to work with, the amount Jackie felt the Lord would have him pay for it. The publican wanted four thousand. However, after a couple of weeks of haggling, or as business men prefer to call it, negotiation, it was eventually bought at Jackie's price, two thousand.

Because of the events of the past six months and the hitherto weakness of my faith I had decided not to take part in any public witness for a time. I felt it better to wait until I had proved the Lord some more - and until he had proved me. It would be better to be sure that the Lord was opening doors for me than to rush in at every opportunity. Too often in the past I had been more keen to get into the limelight than to achieve something constructive and honouring to God.

In fact, shortly after this decision had been made I was put to the test when an invitation came from a christian businessman's association. However, still feeling it was much better to wait until the right moment and until I was ready, I declined.

That's not to say I wasn't willing to do whatever the Lord would have me do, no matter how difficult. I was willing to tackle anything he wanted even if it seemed impossible and I told the Lord as much. I didn't have to wait very long before he confronted me with the ultimate test.

For a number of weeks the New Lodge Road and Ardoyne districts of Belfast had been weighing heavily on my mind. For those who don't know about them these are two of the most staunchly Roman Catholic areas of the city.

139

They are also nationalist and republican strongholds - and 'no-go' areas for protestants and particularly so for an ex-UVF man like me. Even the police force patrol only in armoured cars.

However I kept thinking back to that day when I had laid my little daughter to rest in Milltown cemetery. The spiritual darkness of those precious Roman Catholic souls had been burned into my heart and it seemed as if God was telling me to go and bring them the good news of the gospel - of a full and free salvation through Jesus Christ. A salvation, not of works, not by church membership, not through ritual - but by simple faith in the Son of God.

Shortly after that I made my first visit into the Ardoyne area with a handful of gospel tracts. Three of us started out on the journey that day but by the time I reached Ardoyne I was alone. The other two had taken fright and decided to put into practice the old saying, "Discretion is the better part of valour!"

It didn't take me long to realize that God had given the vision for these areas to me - and not necessarily to others. This would be a lonely mission.

But that didn't matter. The Lord himself had promised to be with me and I was going forth at his command. The soldier doesn't ask the commander to explain the orders - he just obeys them.

Up until the time of writing I have been in one or the other of these districts about twenty times, mostly alone and each time I have returned unscathed. On three occasions other believers have plucked up the courage to come with me, one at a time, but for each of them, once was enough. And yet they all returned home again quite safely because, in the words of a former American president, "There is nothing to fear but fear itself!" Perhaps the book of Proverbs puts it even better - "The fear of man brings a snare!"

Now I don't want you to get the idea that I'm some kind of super hero - a spiritual Rambo who knows no fear. I'm not. I've had my share of frightening experiences over the years. I remember giving out tracts in a block of flats one morning at about seven o'clock.

Suddenly, behind me, I heard the sound of a door opening and when I turned to look the occupant, a man who had obviously just received one of my tracts and didn't think much of it, shouted abuse and threats at me. I did what I thought was the sensible thing, not necessarily the brave thing, I took to my heels and ran! "No point in talking to a man who doesn't want to listen," I thought.

It took me about ten minutes to get my breath back and, along with that came the courage to go back and finish the job. I delivered all those tracts praying all the while for God to protect me. Someone once defined courage like this. It's not the absence of fear - but being able to overcome fear! I believe God gave me an abundance of courage that day.

The first six months living in Ballysillan saw me very busy, with usually not enough time to do all the things asked of me.

I had started to train for the Belfast city marathon, running not just for the good of my health, but to raise sponsorship money for Youth for Christ. I really did train hard for the run and managed to finish it too, albeit in a very slow time. Twenty-six miles is a long hard struggle, even for the fittest of men, but I was pleased to complete the course and Youth for Christ benefited to the tune of nearly three hundred pounds.

I'm pleased to say also that during all this time my relationship with the Lord went from strength to strength. I was becoming physically and spiritually fit at the same time.

There is no doubt in my mind that the reason for the spiritual strength was the amount of time that was being given to Bible study. Whatever had happened on that night when I listened to the W.P. Nicholson tape had left me with a tremendous hunger to know more of God. That hunger was manifested in my appetite for his word.

In those days I thought nothing of sitting down for three hours at a time and just perusing God's word. I got great help, too, through a set of cassette tapes I had bought.

Remember I hadn't received much of an education and my reading left a lot to be desired. But these tapes were great. I would recommend them to anyone with the same problem. The tapes contained the whole of the Authorised version of the Bible, beautifully and clearly read.

I just sat there and read along with them, sometimes playing the same section over again, two or three times, to make sure I had got it right. Using this method I was able to master the correct pronunciation of difficult words, like place names, and it also helped me to commit the better known passages to memory.

At the same time I also developed a passion for good theological books, and in this was greatly helped by John Greer, the manager of a Christian book-shop in downtown Belfast. On many occasions John gave me sound and helpful advice on Christian books and guided me in stocking my humble but sufficient library. For this I'll always be grateful to him.

Of course, the only real time I had for study was in the evenings for during the day I was still employed in the Elim ACE scheme. I was very grateful for the job but, as time went on, I became more and more discontented. Office work wasn't one of my strong points and I hated all the paper work associated with the job. It was all quite boring and I longed to be free of it.

However, I had arranged to go and see Eric Lennon, the Director of the Shankill Road Mission. He was to provide some statistics on homelessness in North and West Belfast.

You'll remember Eric Lennon from earlier in the book. He was the man who came to see me when I worked in CCV Helps and who came to the conclusion, rightly at the time, that I was a pompous, big headed, know it all.

Eric greeted me with some degree of caution this time around but after a little while he confessed to seeing a great change in me. I had been broken and remade and the transformation was clear to see. So impressed was he with what the Lord had done that he again asked if I'd be interested in taking a job at the Mission.

We chatted about the prospect for a while and then he decided to set up an interview for me that very afternoon. It wasn't possible for him to conduct the interview because he knew me so well and would possibly be biased in my favour so he arranged for two other people, Orville Webb, the mission manager, and Davy McClure, its project leader, to do it.

The interview was tough, to say the least, even a bit harsh at times I thought. It left me quite drained mentally but, at the end of it, I was given verbal confirmation that the job was mine if I wanted it I and could start on the following Monday week.

My first day at the mission was spent getting to know the others who worked there. I wasn't the only new start; there was another chap called Raimey who was as new to this kind of work as I was. He was the drummer in a rock gospel band called "Noah's Ark," but like me, he needed a day job too and so he came to work at the mission. He and I became very good friends and sometimes it must have been quite funny watching us helping each other out over things we weren't sure about. It must have been like the blind leading the blind.

The Shankill Road Mission was an old established christian work, dating back to the last century and the days of the old Albert hall. In the twenties the mission had played host to such preachers as W.P. Nicholson who was instrumental in bringing thousands to Christ. Nicholson's ministry in Northern Ireland is well known and well documented; there are plenty of books and pamphlets about it.

Most of the mission's original building, The Albert Hall, was pulled down years ago. Only the front portion remains and that was the mission's entire premises until a new extension was added a few years ago. The extension provides recreational space for such things as snooker, table tennis and a coffee bar.

All this is done to help meet the needs of people in an area of high unemployment, and gives them both physical and mental outlets.

Of course, the overall plan is to reach individuals with the saving message of Jesus Christ and, in a modern age, modern methods must be employed to attract men and women to where the gospel is proclaimed. That's why the Shankill Road Mission was formed in the first place.

The mission was normally open five days a week and provided a number of services, including day centre and cafe, where good food was provided at reasonable prices. When I was there about forty people used the place regularly every day. Most of these were unemployed and many had special needs like homelessness and alcoholism. Others were just depressed and in need of company. It was our job to help them in whatever way we could and oftentimes it wasn't easy.

Most of the fellas who came into the mission were staunch loyalists, a few were paramilitaries too, and felt they had some kind of reputation to uphold. This often led to problems, now and again of a serious nature.

For instance, one day one of these lads came in and Michael, a new worker who didn't know the score, said something to him which was taken the wrong way. Before we knew it a battle of words had broken out and a battle of fists didn't seem too far away. This paramilitary guy wanted to fight and what was worse - he wanted to fight me. After pelting me with a volley of verbal abuse, he invited me outside, to the car-park, where the matter could be settled - and by the size of him, probably in his favour.

I don't mind telling you I was frightened - not only of the fella - but of myself. His personal abuse didn't bother me too much, I could forget that. But I was amazed at my own anger and quickness of temper. I think if he had tempted me much longer I'd have out to that car-park and who knows what the outcome would have been?

It was an extremely frustrating episode, and all the more so for me because it wasn't my fault. I was just the guy in the middle, trying to pour oil on troubled waters. The real truth is that, this guy just couldn't stand christians and it seemed that, as far as he was concerned, I was in the wrong place at the wrong time.

Worst of all, the incident left a bad taste in mouths for quite a while. Every time he came into the centre, for days afterwards, he gave me dirty looks and made sarcastic remarks. It got so bad that, in the end, I dreaded coming to work because I didn't know what outburst to expect from him.

Finally, however, the Lord put me right and I realized he was just the kind of person Christ died for. From then on the grace of God upheld me and kept me from loosing my cool. Davy McClure was a good help too. By this time he and I had become good friends and I was able to confide in him over the matter.

There were many other incidents similar to that one, although none of them were as near to ending in fisticuffs. However, each one was a learning experience, each one taught me something new about life and people, and each one strengthened my faith.

The Lord had not put me in the Shankill Road Mission just to serve him. He put me there to educate me and to prepare me for what lay ahead. Every experience, every conflict with the enemy, taught me more than volumes of books ever could.

As well as that I was working with two great men in Eric Lennon and Orville Webb. Their patience, their love and kindness toward me are things I'll never forget. The debt I owe them for their practical and spiritual counsel is something I'll never be able to repay. However, the Lord says of them, "I know thy works." He will abundantly repay them.

CHAPTER FIFTEEN

THE WHITEWELL INFLUENCE

*"STUDY TO SHOW THYSELF APPROVED UNTO GOD, A
WORKMAN THAT NEEDETH NOT TO BE ASHAMED, RIGHTLY
DIVIDING THE WORD OF TRUTH."*
2 TIMOTHY 2 v 15.

At the time I left the Elim ACE scheme to go and work
with the Shankill Road Mission, I also made another
important decision. It regarded my attendance at Ballysill-
lan Elim Church.

The church seemed to be going through some changes
and these, whether right or wrong I'm not judging, had a
direct affect on me.

Pastor Jackie McKee was now busier than ever. As well
as being the church's pastor, he was also Irish national
Youth Director for Elim. And now he had taken on yet
another responsibility, that of manager of the Stadium
Youth Centre, at the top of the Shankill Road.

The Stadium was originally a cinema, but then, in the mid
1970's, Belfast City Council turned it into a sports com-
plex. However, for reasons best known to themselves, the
council decided to sell it to the Elim movement who
continue the sporting activities and also use it as a christian
conference centre. Jackie McKee is now the manager
there.

With all this added burden on his shoulders, he was less and less in the pulpit on Sundays. Other people took his place and I missed his valuable and instructive ministry.

There were changes, too, in the youth movement in the church. It seemed that all my companions were pairing off with girl-friends and I was being left almost alone. Naturally, I felt a little bit left out of things.

Now I'm not blaming anyone for this. That' life. Young people grow up, form relationships with members of the opposite sex, get married, start families of their own, settle down and suddenly discover they have less time for their friends. It's not that they shun their old friends, it's just that new, more important priorities take precedence.

It was probably an awkward stage I was going through, but it meant that I no longer felt as much a part of the church family in Ballysillan as I had, hitherto. I must add here that I bear them no grudge. The people in Ballysillan were absolutely marvellous to me, as I've recorded earlier in this book, and they will always have a special place in my heart. But, as I say, changes were taking place and these changes forced me to look elsewhere for fellowship. As it happened, the place I found came to me - and more by providence than by searching.

One day, in the Shankill Mission, as I sat talking to Davy McClure he invited me to his house for tea.

"In fact, why don't you come tonight?" he said. "And if you've nothing else arranged, why not come along with me to our Bible study as well?"

It was a Wednesday, and there would be nothing on that night at the Elim, so I decided to take him up on the offer.

When I walked in to Davy's church that Wednesday night it was just as I had remembered it from four years earlier. The only thing different about it was the name. When I had gone there, it was the Whitewell church of God. Now it was the Metropolitan Church, Whitewell Road.

You'll remember that it was through two young Whitewell members, Sam Loughran and Robert Long, that I had first learned of God's love for me.

I had attended the church for a couple of months at that time and had made a lot of friends there. As I walked through the doors that night I wondered how many of them I'd meet again; how many of them had prayed for me these past four years and how they'd react when I told them of all the Lord had done for me in that time. I especially wanted to see big Sam Loughran. He, above all people, had been a great source of encouragement to me.

The meeting was like a breath of fresh air to me and I thoroughly enjoyed myself. The presence of God was evident throughout the service and I was lifted heavenward all the while.

The high point of the evening was the Bible study. It was conducted by one of Pastor McConnell's young assistants, David Purse, who spoke on the judgment seat of Christ. Although David Purse is still only in his mid-twenties, he has a tremendous grasp of the Word of God and he preached that night with a heavenly anointing. He's a young man whom God obviously has great plans for.

I left the meeting and went home totally refreshed. Truly God had blessed me in that place; it had been a Bethel to me - a house of God. So, when Davy asked me the following Wednesday if I'd accompany him again, I jumped at the opportunity.

This time Pastor McConnell conducted the Bible class himself; he was just commencing a series of studies on Mark's gospel. Hearing him preach again did something special for me. It was like touching an old nerve, only in a pleasant sort of way. It had been years since I'd heard him, and that night I sat up and listened intently. Pastor McConnell was the first real gospel preacher I'd ever heard and during the couple of months I'd gone to the church then, his ministry had done a lot for me. As well as that, Whitewell was the first church I had regularly attended, so there was still quite a bond with the place and an affection for Pastor McConnell. Surprisingly, all this left me very confused.

I was strongly drawn towards Whitewell but still had a great love for Ballysillan Elim. They had been there when I needed them most and even when I let them down, they were still there. The very thought of deserting my spiritual home horrified me but I was inexorably drawn to Whitewell. What a decision faced me! It wasn't going to be easy.

I realised that whatever decision I made, it would be a long term one. I would have to live with it. There could be no turning back. Also, the wrong decision would have a disastrous effect on me spiritually. So there must be no mistake.

Well, there's only one way to make a decision like that - by prayer. I took a long time to pray about it. In the book of James God promises, "If any of you lacks wisdom, let him ask of God, who gives to all liberally and without reproach, and it will be given to him." (James 1 v 5.)

I claimed that promise, again and again, and eventually felt led to sever my connections with Ballysillan Elim and throw in my lot at Whitewell.

The decision was tough in the end and many tears were shed over it. I was sorry to be leaving those people who had done so much for me and whom I'd grown to love and respect. However, my mind was made up. I sat down and wrote the letter of resignation to the friends in Ballysillan.

Pastor McKee was the one person I thought would be hardest to tell but, as usual, he was sympathetic and understanding. We chatted about the matter for quite some time, and once he knew that I was clear about what I was doing, he wished me God's blessing. He had given me tremendous help over the past two years, and now he was wishing me well as I moved on in my earthly sojourn. I'll always respect him for that.

The next few months in Whitewell turned out to be a time of abundant blessing for me. Pastor McConnell's preaching struck home, like an arrow, to my heart, and his teaching fed me and strengthened me continually.

He's a man who leads by example and his own personal testimony and walk with God never ceased to inspire me. In his autobiography, Pastor McConnell remarks how he finds it much easier to pray as he walks along. That encouraged me a lot, because I do that too and have been doing it for years.

As a result of all this my prayer life increased, as did my relationship with the Lord. I was greatly burdened for people I had never even met and the Roman Catholic areas of Belfast were constantly on my mind. The normal bitterness I had towards Roman Catholics was removed and I longed for them to come into the same experience of God's salvation that I knew.

Something wonderful was happening in my life and I was enjoying every minute of it. The Lord was maturing me through his word and I was hungry for it. Whitewell was a great place to be in those days. Pastor McConnell, affectionately known as, "The Bishop," always had fresh bread for his people every Sunday. You could be guaranteed of that.

To complement the instruction that was coming from the Whitewell pulpit, I did a lot of reading on my own. Someone had lent me a television set but after a few weeks I returned it, deciding that more thorough study, without hindrances, would be much more beneficial. I was continually collecting books and reading the great christian authors like C.H Spurgeon, F.F. Bruce and A.W. Pink.

There was a period of about five months when I didn't bother with anyone. Except for work during the day, church on Wednesday evening and Sunday, I hardly ever saw a soul. I just closed myself in and spent my time reading my books and seeking God. A lot of my friends thought I was going crazy and on more than one occasion told me to slow down. However, they needn't have worried. God had me in his school and I was well under control.

CHAPTER SIXTEEN

OPPORTUNITIES

"BEHOLD I HAVE SET BEFORE THEE AN OPEN DOOR."
REVELATION 3 v 8.

During those long months, which were spent alone, in search of knowledge and gospel truth, there were many times when I had grave doubts about my future. Would God ever use me again? Was there a work for me to do? Had I blown my last chance of serving in his kingdom?

Then I remembered Samson. He had broken his vows of consecration and despised the calling of God. Yet, in the prison grinding house, his eyesight gone and a slave to God's enemies, the scripture records that, "The hair of his head began to grow again." And as the locks of his consecration returned and he himself repented of his folly, so his great power with God was restored. At last, in the providence of God, he found himself between the pillars of the temple. With a final great cry to Heaven for vengeance on the Philistines for his two eyes, he pushed those pillars apart and the whole temple structure disintegrated. Samson slew more in his death than in all his life.

I remembered Jonah, who fled in the opposite direction when God gave him a work to do. But, as he sailed away on the ship of unbelief and disobedience, God caught up with him and we all know how he eventually ended up in the belly of the great fish. But God didn't leave him there forever. Three days and three nights were enough for Jonah to cool off and realise what a fool he had been. When the fish finally spewed him out on the dry land, Jonah couldn't get to Ninevah quickly enough to take up the challenge God had given him.

I thought, too, about poor Peter. He was so outspoken and brash in his support of the Lord before the crucifixion. Yet when the chips were down, as they say, he crumbled under the pressure and denied the Lord three times. What a miserable specimen he must have felt. I'm sure he tossed and turned in bed at night, fretting over what he had done. Yet, on the glad morning of resurrection, when the two Marys and Salome arrived at the empty tomb in search of the body of the Saviour, they were told by the young angelic messenger, "Christ is not here. He's risen! See the place where he lay. Now go and tell his disciples - and Peter." Despite all his denial's Peter was singled out for special mention and he went on to become one of the Lord's greatest servants.

I remembered, too, that God uses broken things. Not many wise, not many mighty, not many noble are called. But God has chosen the foolish things, the weak things, the base things and the despised things ..... that no flesh should glory in his presence.

When I considered all of this, I felt that God was not finished with me yet. The weeks and months of study and preparation would not be in vain. When God's time was ripe, the openings and opportunities would come - and they did.

All of a sudden, the invitations began to pour in from all over the country. Local churches, youth clubs, coffee bars, even schools wanted to hear my story and asked me to come and tell it.

My testimony was printed in a presbyterian magazine, "The Christian Irishman." It has a circulation of over ten thousand and a readership of more than twice that number. I wrote that article very prayerfully and God has been pleased to bless it to many. It also became the basis for the introduction to this book.

Going around the schools has presented me with the biggest challenge of all. Young people are great. They are the nation of the future and so inquisitive too. They always want to ask lots of questions and sometimes these can be quite personal and tricky to answer.

For example, if you were me, how would you respond to questions like these?

"If you hadn't got caught do you still think you would be a Christian?" "Do you think if you hadn't got God you might have killed someone?" "Do you have anything to do with the paramilitaries now?"

These are tough questions and I hope I answered them honestly and wisely.

"If I hadn't spent time in prison I hope I would still have become a Christian. It's a great life." "I sincerely hope I wouldn't have killed anyone. But men without Christ can fall into the deepest of sins and are capable of anything." "Once my former paramilitary associates heard that I was a Christian they had no more time for me. They wished me well. We parted company and I have no longer any involvement with them."

Despite the difficult questions, the school-room is a great place to put the gospel across. Boys and girls are just as much in need of salvation as older people and I love to tell them of Jesus. In fact that's my main reason for being there.

I would guess that about ninety per cent of the young people I come across are unsaved and yet the response to the message of Christ is tremendous. Between the ages of thirteen and eighteen, young people are probably more open to the gospel than at any other time in their lives. There have been plenty of statistics published to prove this.

One of the strangest meetings I ever spoke at was at the University of Ulster's Jordanstown campus. I thought I was going along to speak to a small group of students but, when I got there, about one hundred and twenty people were packed into the lounge bar. Two thirds of them were members of the Christian Union, the rest were casual lunch time drinkers.

When I was confronted with this scene I was in two minds about whether or not I should speak. However, a chat with the leader put my mind at rest and I decided to give it a go. Most of the unsaved who were there were non church goers so they might not get a chance to hear the gospel again for a long time, if ever.

They had arranged two half hour sessions with another half hour break between the two. I gave it everything I had, putting heart and soul into giving my testimony and then concluding with this story from my days in prison.

A christian prisoner stopped another prisoner in the corridor one day and quite calmly said to him, "I'm sorry to hear about the death sentence you've been put under."

The prisoner immediately panicked and, since capital punishment is no longer the law in Northern Ireland, came to the conclusion that he was on some paramilitary death list. He began to reel off the names of several local commanders, asking which one had put the finger on him and marked him out for execution.

The christian stood silently as the other man enquired, name by name, if so and so was the one who had pronounced sentence upon him. Eventually, in utter frustration, the condemned man begged to be told who had it in for him.

The Christian looked hard and long at him and then quoting from the Bible said, "The wages of sin - is death!"

At this the unsaved prisoner sneered and said, "Is that all you wanted to say to me?" Then he turned to walk away.

But the christian prisoner came back with, "The trouble with you my friend is that your priorities are all wrong. When you thought that someone in here was going to put the finger on you and have your life extinguished, you were ready to crawl around these cells on your hands and knees begging for mercy. The fact is, there is one who is able to cast both body and soul into Hell and you refuse to bow the knee to him. Yes, your priorities are all wrong."

I went on to conclude my message to the students by explaining how, very often in life, we get our priorities all wrong. We are so keen to satisfy the physical and material needs of life that we neglect the spiritual. And yet life is so short and so uncertain - eternity is so long and so sure.

The Lord gave me great liberty that day at the University and the crowd gave me a good hearing. It was both a thrill and a privilege to tell out the good news of salvation to those who might never hear from anyone else.

However, I can't lay enough stress upon the fact that a meeting of that nature shouldn't be attempted unless there's been much prayer beforehand. In fact, it should go without saying that no ministry should be undertaken without much prayer.

Someone once said, "We must learn to talk to God for men, before we dare talk to men for God!" How true that is. If a preacher can't take time to wait upon the Lord before he stands behind the sacred desk, then he should never presume to stand there in the first place. If he does, he is wasting his own time and the time of his hearers also, for God will not anoint a prayerless ministry.

The greatest possible privilege a preacher can have is the joy of leading another soul to Christ. The Lord has been good to me in this respect. I have had the joy of seeing many come to Him.

157

I remember once, at a meeting in a church near Bally-mena, a young woman coming to me after the service and saying, "My friend's down there. She's weeping and would like to speak to you."

She led the way to where her friend was sitting and I sat down with them both and explained the way of salvation, as simply and clearly as I could. When I had finished the young woman who had first spoken to me said, "I'm not saved either but I'd like to be."

We all knelt down together and they both prayed the sinner's prayer, "Lord, be merciful to me a sinner." Afterwards, the tears of repentance and joy rolled down their cheeks as they experienced the peace of the new born child of God. What a thrill it was for me to be instrumental in their conversion. And what joy there must have been in their homes later that night as they told their parents of how Christ had met them. They both came from Christian homes. No doubt their mothers and fathers had prayed for them from birth and now their prayers had been wonderfully answered.

At this point I can't resist a, "Praise the Lord!" How I wish I could be there with you to shout it. It's such a thrill to see precious souls coming to Christ and even now it does my heart good to tell it again. The Lord certainly knows the best medicine for his oft' discouraged servants.

During all this time of public ministry I have received a lot of help from a great many people, but one man in particular stands out, my old friend the Rev. Jackson Buick.

You'll remember that he was the prison chaplain in the Crumlin Road when I was there. Since then he has been transferred to the chaplaincies of the Maze and Magahaberry prisons, both near Lisburn.

Rev. Buick has kept in touch with me since my release from prison and has taken a keen interest in my progress. He regularly invites me to his home and advises me on any problems I encounter in my own ministry. With thirty years experience behind him he's just the man to guide a young apprentice like me. He's also been responsible for putting a lot of speaking opportunities my way. Apart from all this, he's a great personal friend and a man I have a lot of respect for.

Of course, along with all the blessing that's come my way there are problems too. When you're on the front line for the Lord, you can expect Satan to hit you with whatever he can. But despite the persecutions and tribulations which are the lot of the christian soldier, I've managed to keep battling on. Every trial only serves to draw me closer to my Lord and to make me stronger in the end.

Gold tried in the fire is the purest and the most valuable. In the same way the Lord allows his saints to be purified in the fires of men's opposition. Indeed he says, "I have chosen thee in the furnace of affliction." How else can the dross of our old nature be removed but by the heat of the fire.

I suppose it's fair to say that I have been attacked by the Devil at almost every meeting I've addressed, and yet the Lord has brought me through it all, victoriously. In the words of a well known gospel hymn, "There's victory in Jesus."

CHAPTER SEVENTEEN

THE HAPPY ENDING

"SEEK YE FIRST THE KINGDOM OF GOD AND ALL THESE THINGS SHALL BE ADDED UNTO YOU."
SCRIPTURE REFERENCE NEEDED

There were more benefits to attending the church at Whitewell than just good Bible teaching, as I was soon to discover.

As you've read this book you'll have realised that, basically, I've been a very lonely man all my life. As a child I had no brothers or sisters to play with. In my youth, whilst I had a large number of acquaintances, few of them could be called real friends, in the true sense of the word. Prison is not the ideal place to establish lasting friendships and since I had been released, the only friends I'd made were in the churches I'd attended. But even then, they were arm's length relationships.

Ever since I'd been restored to the Lord I had purposely steered away from the company of girls. It's not that I dislike girls, far from it, but remember I'd had a couple of disastrous relationships, one a marriage which had failed. That made me rather wary of future entanglements. In fact, as far as I was aware, I was still married. The divorce which Michelle was suing for still hadn't been finalised and I didn't feel it would be right to get involved with anyone else until it was.

About six months after I'd been released from Crumlin Road I decided to telephone the solicitor to see what news he had of the divorce settlement. To my absolute surprise he informed me that I'd been divorced for about six weeks. As you can imagine, I was dumbfounded. Why had no-one told me?

However, as I thought about it, I felt that perhaps this was the Lord's way of saving me from any further emotional strain.

Michelle had hurt me so many times in the past, the most recent when I'd written to her expressing how sorry I was for the pain I had caused her. Marriage break downs are very rarely the fault of one partner and I had come to realise that I was to blame for a lot of the problems between Michelle and myself. I was truly sorry for that and wanted to make amends. I believed I still loved her too, and wanted us to be together again. So I wrote the letter.

The response I got was a reply from her solicitor warning me not to make any contact again. If I did I would be liable for prosecution.

About a month after I got the news that the divorce was final, I got talking to a young woman in Whitewell church. She was very pretty and introduced herself as Margaret. Along with her she had an equally pretty young daughter called Naomi. Margaret was a single parent and had been a christian for just nine months. She confessed that she was finding it difficult to understand a lot of things. I admitted that I didn't have all the answers either but was willing to help in any way I could.

Margaret and I became friends very quickly, and over a period of a few weeks a more serious relationship began to develop. But there were problems. There wasn't just the matter of getting to know Margaret there was the problem, and it was a problem, of getting to know her daughter Naomi, too.

Naomi was just turning four years old and up to this time, had been used to the undivided attention of her mother. I suppose the child looked upon me as something of an intruder and felt threatened by my regular presence in the home. Sometimes she would come out with things that were quite embarrassing to us both.

"Are you going home yet?" "This is my mammy's flat. You're not coming to live here, are you?"

I suppose both of us should have been able to handle remarks like these. After all, she was only a child of four. But they did make us feel a bit uncomfortable at the time.

Margaret also had a fourteen year old son, called Stephen. For the past three years he had been in the care of the Social Services, because Margaret had found him rather difficult to control on her own. Acting on the advice of the welfare authorities, she had agreed to having him placed in a home for young people where he could be better disciplined and looked after. She, of course, visited him a couple of times every week and he also had access by telephone if there was anything he needed.

Despite this the relationship grew and blossomed into true love. As a matter of fact it happened so quickly that neither of us could believe it. And since we had both come from previously disastrous relationships, we were all the more careful and wary of what was happening.

I suppose in modern terms our courtship was a strange one. Instead of spending our time together walking hand in hand along romantic lanes, we spent it mostly in Margaret's flat, talking about the Lord and reading the Bible.

We took it in turns to read a chapter of God's word out loud and before long we had read right through the New Testament. Following the reading, we knelt together in prayer. In this way our relationship grew on a higher spiritual plane.

I remember, just about two weeks before I met her, asking the Lord for a girlfriend who would be totally surrendered to him. In Margaret those prayers were abundantly answered. She may have complained that she lacked knowledge, but she certainly made up for that in sheer enthusiasm. She was so keen to learn; so anxious to do what was right in God's sight. Above all, her heart was in the right place.

Eventually, we decided to get married and arranged an interview with the pastor, Irwin Rea, one of the assistants at Whitewell. He had been very helpful when I went to him for advice, just after meeting Margaret. I wasn't sure whether it was right to keep company with her, since I was a divorcee. However, he assured me that since it was my ex-wife who had left me and since it was she who had sued for divorce, there was nothing unscriptural or wrong in my wanting to marry again.

Along with Irwin Rea we sorted out the details of the wedding and set the date for the third of November 1989.

In the few weeks leading up to the wedding it was amazing how the Lord made provision for all our needs. Neither of us had very much money to spare and yet there were so many things that we needed. However, a suit for me, an outfit for Margaret, a wedding cake and a wedding car were all provided, from different sources, by good Christian friends who were happy for us and wanted to help us.

The wedding itself was a fairly quiet affair with just twenty-six guests, all immediate family or friends, and it was held in the Metropolitan Church at Whitewell, where we first met. Pastor Irwin Rea performed the wedding ceremony and preached to us from Psalm 23 on, "The Lord is my Shepherd."

There was a simple reception afterwards in a downtown restaurant and eventually, Margaret and I drove off into the sunset as man and wife.

From the very beginning the Lord has blessed our married life together and of course, we have always sought it. On the day we arrived back home after the wedding, the first thing we did was to kneel down together and re-commit ourselves to him. I'm sure you've often seen those motto cards hung up in many an Ulster home which proclaim, "Christ is the head of this house. The unseen guest at every meal. The silent listener to every conversation."

That's how we wanted it to be in our new home.

At the beginning Naomi found it a bit strange having me around the house all the time. It took a bit of adjustment on her part, but eventually, she accepted me all right. I'll never forget the first time she called me, "Daddy." You can imagine how thrilled I was. I had grown very attached to her over the past few months and felt that she filled the gap left by the death of my own little daughter a year previously.

Margaret's son, Stephen, and I have also become quite close. He looks upon me as a big brother and I'm very proud of that. We spend quite a bit of time together, meeting on Saturday afternoons to play snooker. Stephen usually beats me. The four of us are becoming closer as a family and, hopefully, Stephen will soon be home with us too, completing the family circle.

Margaret has proved to be a tower of strength to me in my ministry, supporting me and encouraging me. She's also very understanding when I have to go away to conduct meetings all over the country. For all that she has been to me since we met, I have to thank her - and praise God.

I cannot conclude this account of the Lord's dealings with me, without a final request to you, the reader. The Lord has been gracious and merciful to me. Like the

Psalmist I can testify, "He brought me up also out of an horrible pit, out of the miry clay, and set my feet upon the rock, and established my goings." (Psalm 40 v 2.)

If you're a Christian, rejoice with me in the Lord's goodness, and pray for my ministry in the future.

However, if you're not yet a believer in the Lord Jesus I've a last word for you as well. What God has done for me, he can also do for you. He is no respecter of persons and if you, as I did, cry to him for mercy and for the forgiveness of sins, he will hear your call.

Recognise that you are a sinner and that you cannot save yourself. Repent of your sins. That is, turn from them and turn to Jesus Christ. Receive Christ as your saviour by simple faith. Believe his promise,

"If we confess our sins, he is faithful and just to forgive us our sins and to cleanse us from all unrighteousness." (1 John 1 v 9.)

Finally, confess Christ to others.

"With the heart man believeth unto righteousness and with the mouth confession is made unto salvation." (Romans 10 v 9.)

May God bless you all, and if don't happen to meet in this world may we meet, through Christ, in the world to come.